Sowa's Red Gravy Stories
(Southern Mudbone Wisdom)

By

Diane Richards

In memory of

Zora Neale Hurston

(HarlemRenaissancePublishing.com)

ISBN: 0-7596-4269-9

This book is printed on acid free paper.

1stBooks – rev. 04/18/02

Table of Contents

I. Introduction

Let me say right off I'm a witch living in the spirit. Nevertheless, I don't follow that devil man. I don't have nothing to do with that old thang. I'm just an old woman who believes in mother nature. So there. And I'm proud to be old.

I live up there around 125th Street in Harlem U.S.A. Won't tell you exactly where cause I don't want you searching me out to try and get you some spells or something.

You know some folks so superstitious. They think all they got to do to fix their life up is to gaze into the eyes of a person like me. Well that just ain't true. You got to have commonsense and know right from wrong, and don't set up and watch life pass you by that's what.

I'm currently working through this here writer. She got some sense, but not much. Her heart is good even though she been peculiar since she was born. I'm gwine help her cause she's helping me express myself.

I was getting tired of hanging out with those tired spirit friends of mine. Either they busy stirring up trouble among you living or moaning and groaning cause they can't experience the pleasures of the flesh. Me, well I just smoke my pipe, rock in my chair and mind my own business.

This young gal writer here perked my curiosity with her determination that she a witch and her third eye bein' open to receive good knowledge. Good thang she ain't fooling with those evil spirits cause I wouldn't have nothing to do with that.

I did that once. Nothing but the funkiest of trouble, believe you me. I think this writer's on the path, but she don't know the half of it. She knows I'm a friendly spirit and that's why she's letting me speak through her. But, she's got a evil streak too. You betta be careful gal. Hanna following your every foot step. (I'll tell yah later all about Hanna.)

I visited this child's house and helped her get rid of that Doberman she had ruling her life. What she needed was a man and I helped her with that too. I believe in doing not just setting up, wishing, hoping and dreaming.

All right, now back to you.

What I'm gwine give to you is my stories and some old folk wisdom for the broken hearted, fool hearty and naive. Now you can say you ain't studding me and that will be just fine. But those of you with some sense gwine listen up.

Now about my name. It's pronounced So'wa. Written just so - Σοωα - remind yah of "So What." I like that name cause folks find too much fever on what don't matter anyway. If something worrying yah, just think "So What," that's what.

Can't nobody, even the baddest witch, tell you your future. You remember that. Cause when they come to you telling you what you gwine do, walk away because they're evil.

So you know who you're talking to now. I'm a spirit and if you gon get spooked or think something's wrong with conversing with spirits than you need to put this book on down.

Now, I love to tell fascinating stories. But boy can I tell me some lies! You know, stories that the old folks tell got truth in them. That's right. You'll see for yoself when you get to reading my stories.

I tell stories to help folks relax and forget about their problems. Life ain't that hard chillun when you start laughing instead of crying all the time. But if you want to keep busy making misery won't nobody stop you.

So come on child. Prop those tired feet up, soak them in some red salt. That will work. Or sit on your favorite sofabed. Try to rest your mind now and let me tell yah some red gravy stories.

I hope you'll enjoy 'em.

Sowa

II. Southern Mudbone Wisdom – For Broken Hearted Gals

Ok so your heart is broken. Well we gon have to fix that now, won't we? Most likely it's about some tall dark fine ass snake or short, light ugly ass something. But it's probably over some he.

And we just gon have to fix it cause you ain't meant to be no bleeding heart for nobody no time soon.

Well now let's start with the fact that you're a woman. That's where all the trouble starts. The problem is you've got a heart and you wear it where that man can see it. Even if he's a good hearted man - once he knows he's got you - seen your heart all soft and just a dripping with love for him - well even without his evil intent your heart is going to thump in pain sooner than later because you're a woman. And, you've got that heart.

Everybody can talk long, write sermons and jump up and down but the truth be told you're a broken hearted gal sometime when you fall in love.

Just because you're a woman.

What to do?

Can't tell you what to do. But I'll tell you what I did in my young fine ass days. Lord I kept those fine three leg creatures in heat. Yes I did. Had so many dates on a Saturday night in 1922 that I passed the extra men on to my girlfriends. Yes I did. But those gals were always messing up because they gave those three leg creatures satisfaction too fast quick and in a hurry.

So let me tell you if you relax, get grounded in your female and know what you know, that you're the Queen of

Sheba that man will love you to death. And, with some Red Gravy know how, child you'll have your choice of men and your heart will get to the point where it's tender and full of love for the deserving man but it just won't thump for those contrary, controlling and quivering lipped heart stealers. You'll learn from the likes of Miss. Terrie who said, "Girl your heart just can't be that broken no more, no how."

But if you crave that kind of man, Red Gravy know-how will help with that kind too. So take heart child. You'll feel better, your heart will be mended and whole and you'll have the love of your life in no time, that man you're with or someone else. It's up to you.

Story One: White, Yellow, Red and Green (Otherwise known as Candleburnin')

Now if you want to be effective at what yah do, you got to burn candles with religious intent. Yes you do. The color of the candle means something too. White candles keep your spirits in cahoots with the good preventing evilness from walking in and taking over. White candles purify everything that a dark spirit could take a liking to. Dark spirits won't want to linger long where light is shining and taking its time. Yellow candles help your personal power; you got to have your own power strong to stand up for yoself. You just can't go out in the world weak cause the devil just waiting for yah. Red candles stand for love and passion. If you don't have strong feelings about thangs, you tend to neglect 'em. And we can't tell all about love just right here, too much to tell. Just know if you want to be in love, keep that red candle a glowing. Now green is for growth of all kinds. That includes gardens whether it be fruit, vegetables or people, and of course it means money. If your life ain't growing, it's dying. Get busy here planting seeds child. Get busy.

Now remember white, yellow, red and green...candleburning gal...learn how to burn 'em properly for yo good and the good of all. Make yo own candles or buy 'em from a place that's grounded in good. Don't buy from evil, shady folks setting up on their porch just a talking bout everybody cause those candles gon be carrying their spirit. When you light the candles make sure they are on solid ground and you don't have busy mouthed folks or troubled spirits around. It's best to be alone. And, don't let

1

everybody's eyes set on your work. Do it in private. As yah light the candle say: "I light this candle for good work only and for the good of all, and according to free will. So mote it be." And then you'll be on your way for the day. And the next day you know what to do...right?

Story Two: Charmin' the Snake

The snake don't know nothing because his head is always in the dirt or underneath a woman's skirt. However, chillun, you can't tell a snake that. He believes himself to be Gawd possessing eternal life and the powerful spermcount of a young man. Yes he do. If you feel I'm bitter with men, yah got that right. Even if the man is 114 he want to act like a young Adonis.

Lord Gawd praise your name. I am a Christian witch but Jesus help us when yah go to one of those Baptist churches. Morning, afternoon and night the minister, the deacon, the usher, the choir, and the whole congregation just a busy praising mankind with no mention of woman. What happened to womenfolk in the world?

I want you to know it wasn't always that way. A long time ago when Gawd was a woman just minding her own business, she had a hold of thangs. She used to dust and clean and bake those good buttermilk biscuits for every one. She tended to the whole world and most thangs was fine. She didn't favor the womenfolk either. You see she wasn't hung up on sex. Well but that wasn't good enough for a certain man that sucked his lip in every time that good woman went to blessing folks. He was jealous you know and didn't like that she had all the power. After all he was the man with more privilege - so he thought. Well that busy body man gathered all the skinny legged, short manned men he could find and got busy building trouble against Gawd so that one day she came home and those men had rearranged everything and took over. The woman couldn't even get in her own kitchen. Can you believe that? Those busy bodied thangs had took over the girl's kitchen! Well you know she was mad. She put those no count men out and told them they had to work for the rest of their lives cause she wasn't gone put up with that nonsense no how. So the men started spreading lies and building grievances about who and what Gawd was until today they got everybody fooled that Gawd is a man.

Well you know the truth. Iffen there weren't no womenfolk wouldn't been no Jesus. Now you may think this profane and sacrilegious but I had a talk with Gawd. And, she said, "Ain't nobody ever seen me so why all these folks think I'm packing a penis." Amens. Hello.

Now I know you thought I was going to talk to you about charming the snake and I know yah think that snake is your man.

First you got to accept that your man is a snake or nearly a snake or about to be a snake or prone to be a snake. Now what do snakes do? Well, they love dirt! The more dirt, the wetter the better?! They just love to roll around in it, eat it, sleep in it and nest in it. So be clear about who and what yah dealing with. You need to be a snake charmer if you gwine tangle with the snake.

A snake charmer don't waste time doubting herself because when that snake get ready to strike she's ready for him. A snake charmer is her own best friend. If you ain't your own best friend, change up, that's what! If you got nappy hair, be glad you got some hair to be nappy about.

I don't care what nobody says. Varicose veins, cellulite, stretch marks, and wrinkles give you character. Best to think of them that way because ain't nothing you can do in the long run. Pamper those feet and put some castor oil on those corns. If you take care of yoself that snake is gonna want to too and while he's smitten with you he will fall under your many charms.

4

Story Three: Mind Yo Own Business

Now let me tell you if you so worried about what somebody else does, you napping on your own affairs. Here tell one day there was two long, ugly snakes in the Garden of Eden. One was a big old woman and the other preyed on women. The one that preyed on women just about had those female snakes in heat every time he slithered by with his fine, snakey self.

Now, the other snake, the big old woman, sat up on his favorite tree branch and gossiped about that fine snake that was getting fever all day long from the women. He was so busy talking about that other snake that one day he stopped talking and looked up and about and it was time for him to die.

The snake minding his own business lived a good life and that big old woman snake minding everybody else's business died having not lived at all.

Story Four: Voodoo, Black Magic and All Kinds of Mess

Now I knew casually an old witch live there over on 113th Street and that St. Nicholas Avenue. This woman was no friend of mine I want you to know. We both were in love with this man so black we couldn't see him at night. His name was Sapphire. Sapphire had the sweetest stuff in the whole entire world. Kid you not, bless his dead soul.

That woman's name was Luwana. Even though I didn't like her I couldn't fool around cause hear tell she was into that Voodoo, Black Magic and all Kinds of Mess. She even had killed off two husbands that didn't do the right thang by her. So when Sapphire came along she was ready for some good loving.

Now by the way those two husbands she had didn't drink or carouse, but here tell they couldn't satisfy that hungry hefa and that's the reason she put Voodoo on 'em and made 'em die so she could make way for another man. One husband turned completely yellow and swallowed his lips throwing up blood. Lord Jesus. And the other one it's too terrible to tell what became of him.

So anyway when I found out Sapphire was fooling around with me and her at the same time I had to cover myself and bury me some menses with special herbs. Then I rubbed that Negro down with funk-you-up mint oil so when he got with her it would stink to high hell. But what can I tell you? It didn't work.

That evil bitch wanted him anyway! Sweet dick Sapphire.

Sapphire came to me one night look like blood was in his left eye. "Baby I think that Luwana done put a spell on me."

Well you know I was through because he wasn't supposed to be playing in her skirts no how. But I loved the fool and decided to find out exactly what she was doing to him.

Now I had a fellow gal on the path; her name was Windy Willow. Windy didn't play that. She was a lesbian and hated men, and from the day her daddy lay with her mama, she was mad. She was sort of sweet on me too. But she still didn't do no magic for men. She was evil. Her magic was always making those men short and wimpy. One man she turned into a woman (but he was glad cause that was his dream anyway).

I said, "Windy child yah got to go around to Luwana's house and find out what she doing to my Sapphire."

"Sowa I just don't know what yah see in those no count, low down men. They don't want nothin' no how. What seed has he planted for yo ass?"

I said, "Now listen girl didn't I do that last favor for yo niece stirrin' up that whole pot of chamomile and licorice to rid her of those invisible lice. You couldn't do it. So hep me with your evil ass."

Windy spit back, "OK, then but don't say I didn't tell yah to leave that Negro alone. That Luwana ain't nobody to play with. Her heart is blacker than the devil and she don't care who she send to hell."

So my friend Windy paid that Luwana a visit one stormy Tuesday night when the moon was on fire and feeling foolish.

As Windy came up on her doorsteps, Luwana was peeping through her window and shouted to her, "Before

7

yah come pass my door Windy Willow tell me what you want. I ain't got no time to play."

Windy snatched back, "Well ain't you the uppity one gal. I's just paying you a sisterly call to see how's you doing."

Luwana smelling trouble hollered, "The hell you is. I think yah snoopin' for that bitch Sowa. And, snoopin' about something tain't none of your business nor that old floosie."

Windy twisted up her face. "Now listen child whatever yah do don't go disrespecting me or getting on my evil side cause you ain't seen no evil until yah mess with me. So get yo last good manners out and invite me in like yah should have in the first place and treat your elder with some heeding."

Luwana knowing she better act decent grunted and then smiled. "Come on in. Windy Willow. Sits right here in my rockin' chair."

Windy walked on in with a roving eye. "No, I prefers that chair right yonder."

"Can I get yah some mulberry tea?"

Windy eyed her. "Nope. Yah likin' to posion me."

"OK. So what's yah want?"

"Like I said I'm callin' on you to see if you's been sleeping proper at night."

"Why's yah worried?" Luwana said her suspicion growing.

"Cause I think somethin' been visiting you at night. A little sparrow told me." Now I know my friend Windy was getting too fit to be tied.

"Is that so? Well to be honest I think that sparrow is that friend of yourn Sowa."

"Maybe," Windy said trying to keep her evilness still.

Luwana snatched her body around and stared at Sapphire as he entered the room.

Sapphire walked into that evil talking room, looked at both of those hefas and turned on his heels back to the safety of his room.

"I see why you want to rid yo house of my ass so fast."

"Like I said that sparrow is Sowa. I want yah to send her a message," said evil ass Luwana.

"Yeah, what's the message?"

Luwana said, "Tell her that storms come in the night like warnings so she betta heed 'em. Sunlight is the fire that will warm her bed until the full moon is no more, and then she'll know a hell second to none if she mess with me or my man."

Windy Willow eyed Luwana for a moment, wiped her face like she was washing it of dirt, took a deep breath and blew it out at Luwana and said, "Hm Hm. I'll tell her for yah. But you take note of this little gal. I don't know why you two women fightin' over that trash in there. Where that comes from there's plenty and much betta trash if that's what you like. But I'll tell yah this much. If you should go to blows with my friend Sowa, watch out for the rain that pours during the day because that's the power that don't give a hoot about nothin' that mess with me or mine."

Windy got up and walked out Luwana's door.

Windy told me all this hefa crap over some hot buttermilk pancakes. That's when I took to cooking my herbs in the blackest skillet I could find. I used plenty of red gravy secret ingredients and evil warding garlic. That floosie Luwana was determined to have Sapphire or kill him and me if she could. But that greasy red gravy stopped all that Voodoo, Black Magic and All Kinds of Mess.

9

Story Five: Old and Sexy

At 110 I still feel sexy. You probably thinking to yoself how can she with gray hair and feeble body still feel sexy. Well if you ask that question yah just don't know what you talking about. First of all sex begins in the mind.

At any moment I can think about the fine men that I done layed with. That brings me right on back into a state of sex. Of course it's betta to have a fine young body and be able to hold on and not lose your wind when you riding the tide. But believe me you can still experience passion and desire for another person.

Love is sweet. And the best sex is when you love somebody. I know.

I seent a woman about 75 plus, a handsome white woman, with clean shining hair and an experienced face. She wore that expensive perfume Joy; smelled all fresh and happy. She had gotten some color and right there written on her face was that she was a sexual, sensual woman still having sex and wanting sex.

Sex warms the blood. Laying down with someone face to face laughing, smiling and really getting underneath their skin real close is SEX-A. Whether that skin be rough or smooth, the touch keep your heart thumping. Yes it do.

Now being old can complicate the matter. Your body starts to have odd aches and pains and women have women problems and men have men problems. And these problems don't go away easily.

I know sometimes the woman ain't as receptive as she used to be. And the man can't do do what he did at 20. But they both want to do it. What to do? You got to find a way. And, there are ways. That's why I'm glad I've studied the craft.

Well, I'll tell you a story. When I was 82 I met me a young, fine man. He was yellow - not my type necessarilee, but he had lips ripe as a berry and I had to have 'em. Now granted I did meet this man in church and he didn't suspect none of my intentions when I invited him over to my house for Sunday brunch. He thought that he was just visiting a nice old elderly church going lady. Well I had something else for him when he came to the house.

You see when you work magic over the years you learn how to change yoself into whatever you want to be. So when this man rang my doorbell, he found a young 50 year old woman (too much work to make myself 20 you know). And I mean I was young and ripe.

So not only did the young man get himself a Sunday meal, he got desert too.

Take heed to this story cause you never know who be setting up in church. And don't think old folks just setting still. If you're old and want to make love, where there is a will, there is a craft.

Story Six: The Great Goddess

I bet you been worshipping a male god all your life. That's why you womenfolk are so nervous and upset; ain't no role model for women. Why don't you close your eyes and imagine a beautiful, nurturing, mother figure as Gawd. Everythang done turned around, right? I bet you feel relaxed and can believe in yoself. I bet you ain't frightened no more.

That male Gawd with a celibate nature ain't real and I'm here to tell you so. Men just ain't that way! So that man ruled church had to go and make those men say they were monks taking vows of chastity when the truth was they didn't want no woman no how. Now have you ever heard of such a mess?

Deceit surely knows how to dress. So a pasty-faced man in a long black dress swinging some burning incense don't necessarily make me think of Gawd. His lips all pursed up and resolute and that salacious grin, hmm. Not a Gawd that's gonna make a difference in womenfolk's life.

Imagine here you are formed in a way in which you can bring life into the world and you're not suppose to be made in the image of the creator. What was that?

All your life you have been told that Gawd is a man. It's depressing. What's empowering for womenfolk is to think of that power as a patient, loving, nurturing woman ready to soothe and love. Don't you want to be taken care of, loved, and understood?

Now this war between the sexes got to do with men running around wanting the power when women the ones running around with those babies for 9 months, suckling them for another five and then raising them for another 30. Now if you can't get no due from this, well what is it?

All the evil talk about witchcraft mess is booty. Women practicing the craft knew how to brew healing teas. They knew how to go out in the woods and bring back herbs that could cure everythang from a whooping cough to syphilis and women and men problems. They didn't need no menfolk running around calling themselves doctors to heal nothing! Besides in those days when a woman was having a baby she didn't want to see no doctor cause he didn't know what the hell he was doing! She didn't relax until that midwife was there. That good woman would lay her cool hands and fresh towels on the woman's brow, rub that belly down with sweet ointment and sing her song. All that doctor did was raise his brow real high and fuss at her for hollering. Shoot! Cost $10.00 too. Send that midwife over a couple jars of homemade apricot jam and that was that! Besides when you saw the midwife coming that's when you could relax and stop hollering cause you knew you were gonna be alright. Yes yah did.

Now if you want to hear even more, back in the day before man started recording history with figures, women use to run everythang. Now, that's the big secret. Women ran everythang and knew everythang. Men worshipped women cause they couldn't figure out how they could have those babies. Now ain't that nothing? Women knew how but they wouldn't tell cause they suspected those men was evil and big old women with no real purpose but to gossip and startup heaps of trouble like in that Garden of Eden.

Anyway those big old women got together, you know those men that should a been born women but ended up men, and plotted against the real women. They just couldn't stand to see the attention childbearing women got for using the secret of life.

They raped, killed and destroyed temples with their fly trapping mouths. Womenfolk had to go underground and that is how witchcraft started.

A true witch don't want nothan' to do with Satan any less any man except to reproduce. Too much mess and trouble. She'll put up with a real fine man that knows how to pleasure her. But honey, slinging tits across a hot stove for some no count man that don't appreciate you ain't no wise woman's purpose in life.

There's more Christian women the brides of devils than herb healing shaman women. Shaman women don't want nothan' to do with menfolk that drink, gamble and carouse.

So after all is said and done, worshipping the great Goddess is worshipping yoself. It gives you ways of being in touch with yoself. All you have to do to feel Goddess is put your feet in some dirt. To see her, look at the sky. To smell her, sniff a flower. To feel secure with her, listen to the voice of an innocent child and you will know the truth of Goddess spirit.

Story Seven: Sapphire

Poor Sapphire. When he found out I had sent Windy over to Luwana's he curled up on my living room sofa and cried like a sick baby.

"Sapphire baby why yah crying like that? I'm gon take care of you for sure. Yah don't have to fear that black stank woman."

"Yah just don't know Luwana.   The woman is poisonin' me and I have to keep going back to her. I don't want to. But I git a cravin' for her so strong in my belly I have to have her. Sowa, don't you see that bitch done put a hoojo on me?"

"I knows that. That's why I want yah to drink this here. When she gits wind of you she is gonna send yah back to me in a thunder storm. Yah watch baby. Now drink this brew."

He drank my bitches brew and went fast to sleep for 12 hours on my sofa. When I woke in the morning he was gone. Believe you me I was terrified then cause I knew my brew didn't have the power I wanted it to have or that man wouldn't went no where.

That was Friday.

Come Saturday morning Windy Willow found Sapphire, pants curled around his ankles, pants belt around his neck in the middle of 125 and Lenox Avenue with traffic driving around his body. When you came up close on him, cause he was naked, your eyes naturally gravitated to that pubic area. That sweet huge you know what of his was just about gone. That woman had got hungry and went to chewing and had changed that man into a eunuch.

15

I was so mad when I found out about my Sapphire that I turned the lights off in my Harlem apartment for two weeks and made the moon go into hiding for three nights in memory of my black knight. Didn't do nothing but burn black candles and one white for my soul. Windy told me to come out of the house for the funeral. But I couldn't because if I saw Luwana I would try to kill her dead on the spot.

Heard tell too that that funeral was full of Sapphire's women, too many to tell who had been pleasured by him. And, that Luwana sat straight up in the front next to his mama.

I was through.

That was Tuesday.

Come Saturday morning when Luwana came back from shopping she opened her door to her kitchen and there was my Sapphire settin' up in her kitchen waiting for her. She burst into a lightning and dust scream, ran down her back porch, tripped over her bitch brewing pots and landed upside down in the water well. Her neck broke and that was all they wrote.

Now don't wonder too long about how and why all that happened cause ain't nothing like a greasy black skillet and some steaming hot red gravy.

Story Eight: Hanna

Hanna came to me in an unusual way and she been dogging my steps ever since. I seent a portrait of her dressed in black Muslim cloth, eyes just a glowing with a stern expression on her face. That portrait was hanging in an old dusty antique shop in Harlem on 124th and St. Nicholas Avenue. When I saw the portrait of her, her eyes followed me around the room and seem to speak to me like she was a distant relative. So I bought the portrait for $100.00. That was in 1935. That was a fortune back then and I could ill afford it.

But now I know Hanna was always around but I couldn't see her, only could feel her. You see she in the spirit world too. We just on different planes and different states. Hanna has been busy protecting me in my different lives. And I must say that child can be mighty evil and is so jealous of me you wouldn't believe it. Shoot her picture is above my sofa in the living room parlor and when menfolk would come a courting they'd take one look at that picture and her eyes would follow them around the room. Let me tell you half the menfolk never called on me again.

Anyway Reggie, a nosy, tobacco chewing spirit I knowed, told me that Hanna was born in 1857, a "half bred" mixed with Indian blood, white and some Negro. She had a fascination with horses. Horses were her best friends and the one creature she would allow close to her. She gon speak to you now. Gwine Hanna, talk to the folks.

"I always was misunderstood. I never liked men. Everyone I knew always wanted somethan' from me. To lay down with 'em, to cook for 'em, have their babies or

17

just to be their servant in everyway. I refused to live like that.

"You see my father was a Mormon minister who got thrown out of the church and his congregation for sleeping with my mama, his house servant, and filling her with child which was me. My mama was Creole from New Orleans. She was beautiful and had escaped from slavery with me. We escaped on a beautiful, pinto pony that we named Sunfire Blue. Blue died shortly after he got us to the Missouri River from exhaustion.

When we got to Missouri, some Mormons took us in. Mama in her Indian ways knew how to grow food and she taught them how to fertilize earth to grow the best crops. The Mormons didn't turn us away, but they didn't accept us either. Many believed my mama to be evil and that she was cavorting with Satan. They spread lies that she rode a black stallion and hollered at the moon. They even begin to appear at different times around our home praying to keep the evil spirits away. Our two wolf dogs, Sheba and Ram, chased those away. My dogs slept wit me even as a little baby.

Mama and I moved in with two old white, kind spinsters named Anna and Sue Renaldson. Anna and Sue were outcasts from Dayton because they were Wiccan, and they were rumored to be lovers. They had a dude ranch and grew their own food from the land. My mama didn't care at the time because I was a baby and we needed protection. Mama turned the other way at their strange habits involving black cats and spellmaking.

I grew up in Miss. Anna and Miss. Sue's home and when my mom died of pneumonia in 1868 I stayed with them until they drowned in 1875 when their boat turned over in the river. Neither one of them could swim. They had willed their home and property to me and I lived on with the house and the horses. I worked the land and raised the horses alone with the help of a freed slave named Domie. He helped me from time to time in exchange for the fresh bread and vegetables I would give to him.

I knew how to work roots and make potions like Aunt Sue and Aunt Anna had. I was determined to stay to myself. After some nosy busy body thought they saw me hollering at the moon one Halloween night, the town folks grew against me. The few times I would ride into town with Hellcat, my black stallion, the towns folk would whisper and huddle together about me. I just stayed to myself and didn't pay them no mind. Besides Domie had told me they were frightened of me.

But there was a wicked preacher named Minister Wright who felt that I owed him something because he kept the towns people from running me out of town. He bought horses from me. I had 13 horses, seven females and six stud males. I sold some ponies to the Union army and made enough money to buy the whole town. Another reason he hated me.

Minister Wright wanted to bed me. He couldn't understand me because I dressed in black all the time. My skin was burnished cooper and I had long straight black Indian hair. I was a full-bodied woman, as I liked my porridge and fresh oven bread with jam. But in those days a poor meated woman meant a sick woman ready to die in childbirth or from farm labor.

Unbeknownst to his wife, children and congregation, Minister Wright grew obsessed wit me to the point where he dreamed of laying with me and killing me afterward so I could not speak out against him. All this came to me in a dream.

He would see me in the town and just stare. I knew he was after me because his evil spirit had visited me and my soul sisters, Sowa and Windy Willow had foretold me.

It was October 13th that Minister Wright came to me. I had sent Sheba and Ram off with the horses to the animal doctor and was alone at home. I was baking bread and mixing my favorite potion of mystic succotash.

He broke into my front door screaming, "I have you now thou daughter of Satan. I'm going to teach you the power of Jehovah."

I ran out the back of my cabin toward the horse barn. Hellcat was there and saw me coming. His head was peering out of the stable door. He started crying when he saw me. The minister caught me by the legs and punched me hard in the head. I went out for a few minutes. When I came to he was untying his pants and had me pinned down to the floor.

"Bride of Satan," he screamed at me. I was fighting him off but he was 300 pounds and I couldn't win. After he shuddered and collapsed on me, he spit in my face, cut off my hair and then slashed my throat.

Hellcat burst out of his stable as the minister slashed my throat and trampled him to death, dragged his body to the open field and began to run with it. Hellcat ran so hard with the minister's head in his mouth, that the head was loosened from the body. But before this, Hellcat tore both of his arms from his body.

The town's people found Minister Wright headless and naked in the middle of town. Some of them said that they saw me walking past him in spirit form, but the truth is that I was back home feeding Hellcat and baking bread.

Story Nine: Hollywood White Woman

Oh yes honey child even though you can't imagine it, I was a Hollywood white wo-man. I was one of those silky thin, blond headed, blue eyed thangs that wore that blood red thick lipstick and white face powder. I was so white you could see me coming in the dark. Yes mam.

And honey I worked being white. That meant a soap sud didn't lay nan one drop on me unless it was lavender oil baby. I did not sweat darling. And when the white men saw me coming, sugar, they started running like flies spread out all over the place to land on me if they could. Cause I had that white woman thang, a rarity that none of them got to have no less see, that is unless they paid sugar and paid they did. And I don't mean no floozie money neither.

Lord, those were the days.

My name was Renee Bonet. I was French and Jewish. No one knew I was Jewish except my maid and the lover I kept hidden away. I used him after being frustrated with those white panting men and limp you know what's. I mean if you want to see a hard one, it's just got to be black. No two ways about it!

So I had me some picture parts in the 1920's. They were memorable like "Heaven's Night." I was the star crossed lover that died in the end a virgin and in love. There was also "Two Faced Charlie" where I was the gangster's girl. I didn't like that much, too much vulgarity and sweating for my taste.

As a Hollywood white woman I loved my beauty days sugar. I constantly had my hair bleached, my eyebrows plucked, facials, body massages, pedicures and manicures

21

and lots of fun shopping on Fifth Avenue in New York and that Rodeo Drive in California with my teacup white poodle and chauffeur in tow.

I stayed a Hollywood white woman through two lifetimes and then I got bored. Not much to make me fantasize about and I missed loving me some black men openly. But that worship by other people was quite "heavenly" as I would once say.

My skin was flawless and I stayed out of the sun. You see you white women today don't know the beauty of white skin. I was so pampered I would have my chauffeur walk down a sunny block with an umbrella over my head. I went swimming naked under moonlight, and I had women lovers too. They always fell too deeply in love with me, but what was I to do? Quite frankly love with women was easier on my fragile body. Less messy and so much more sanitary. To be honest I could do away with the whole sex thing; too much emotion and trouble for so little return.

Although I always had a place to live and money to travel, I never got much wealth on my own. My men kept me. I was a "kept wo-man." That's what a Hollywood White Woman is about. We do nothing but look like a Hollywood white woman. That's the secret. We do nothing. Everythang is done for us. Elizabeth Taylor, Marilyn Monroe, Audrey Hepburn, Sophia Loren...like that you see.

Maybe I'll come back again as a Hollywood black woman. These gals today don't take no mess. They just as fine as they want to be and know it. Hair all weaved, nails done and that bleaching cream do wonders for age spots to even out that skin. I think these Hollywood black women appreciate this pampering much more then the white women. They got sense. They figure as long as that man is bringing home the bacon, they don't much care what he does as long as it ain't in their face. They don't need that neurotic "I love yah darling" every minute of the day. Just keep that honey, money and milk a flowing and they'll be just fine.

Story Ten: Blue Jay Boy - The Finest Boy Yah Ever Done Seen

You poor hearted girls need to hear a story that will perhaps help you from goin' down a deep dark alleyway over some man. Now listen I knew a woman named Sally Sue. Sally Sue was always mending somebody's clothes or cookin' some sick soul some chicken noodle soup or helping some stray animal. She had a peculiar affinity for menfolk in jails. She use to cook up a big batch of ginger sugar cookies and barbecue, sling it over her hips and tote it all the way to that penitentiary 20 miles away from her old shack in Memphis. She'd even walk there cause her father told her she was a fool and he wasn't gone allow her to use up his gas feeding no criminals! Anyway, one day Sally Sue was sittin' on her porch eating some fresh fried chicken when who come shufflin' up her dirt road but a tall, lean, big old blue eyed man named Blue Jay newly released from the Memphis State Pen.

Of course you know she invited big old blue in for some buttermilk biscuits and hot chicken. That boy sat down on her father's kitchen chair and ate up everythang he could lay his eyes on. After he was done eating he asked Sally Sue did she have anythang to drink. Sally Sue pulled out her father's one bottle of peach apple wine saved from World War I and that boy drank up the whole bottle without so much as offering her a drop. Well after he showed his gratitude by eating and drinking her out of a home without even so much as a thank you, he walked out of the house and didn't even tip his hat at her.

The next day Sally Sue told all her friends at the beauty parlor in town where she did hair that she met the man that she was gonna marry. She told 'em he was an adventurous type and for work traveled the world and didn't have much time to linger in any one place. She said he was a man of few words and much action and that she expected in the near future to be moving out of town to some distant big city.

Finally, Sally Sue said that even with all those exciting qualities the reason she was so smitten with this ill mannered man was that his name was Blue Jay Boy and he was the finest boy she done ever seen! Don't you know that that was 1922 and the last time I checked in 1942 she was still waiting for Blue Jay to come on back.

Story Eleven: Witchiness and the Ultimate Negress

Now I have been a witch in Harlem, manless and happy about the whole thing for a long time. I got me a spirit Doberman named Victor. Victor loves him some women, babies and lonely souls. And he's an anti-drug dog too. One time, a reefer head tried to deliver me some packages I ain't ordered. The fool smelled like burnt rubber and Victor knew he'd been smokin' that ghost. Victor took one look at the man, sniffed his shoe, growled and tried to tear the man's foot off. Now the man had a fit cause can't nobody see Victor except me. The reefer head doesn't deliver to me any more.

Where I live folks don't walk except troubled spirits lookin' for their bleeding souls in evil works. My house is full of burning candles and prayers for folks in need and folks who want to wash their spirits through mudbone wisdom. I help folks find what they lost over lifetimes. You got to belong to yoself. You might wanna believe in more than what you see. I know misery is comin', but for a reason. That reason can be found in the mess that comes to fight with the weak part of you. A Negress knows these things. That's just the way we are.

If you worth your weight in old girl wisdom child, you got the makings of a witch and the ultimate Negress. Even though you may be brainwashed to believe your clitoris is powerless over the mighty penis, believe me your contrary man is once down after a strong dose of your womanhood in its full glory. All you slavegirls can become glorious queens if you want to. And, I'm here to tell yah so.

Even though Voodoo just ain't what it used to be, dolls and needles, herbs and evil intention, it's just as powerful. Voodoo for you is owning property even if you manless, being powerful in your own right rather than relying on the powerful.

Whether he's Jamaican, Jew or Gentile, Irish or plain old Negro, or one of those dowop, doorag or hiphop rap men, men give womenfolk trouble with a capital T. Cause they don't know how to act. If it ain't one thang, it's another. Their money problems, or back problems and good Lord their womenfolk problems, either they got too many, too little, the wrong kind, or they are the biggest women you ever done seen.

Sowa is a Negress. That's right and it ain't about color child although that's where it comes from. People beginning to realize that the black women possess strength that don't nobody have but her. That strength comes from passing up misery. That's right baby and you can learn how to have a Negress' soul. A Negress don't let small stuff git her down, instead she go to praying. A Negress doesn't fool too long with men who gon put her down. She just tells him he got to go and put her foot down. A Negress loves babies and kisses them on their wet behinds and nurses them when they are sick. And, if you put a Negress in a room full of crying babies they will all stop crying because they know love is on the way.

The Negress is the original healer woman. When white men were shining up their knives because they love to cut when somebody sick, the Negress went right on out in the woods and picked her some herbs. She healed sick folks with herbs and her spirit. She knew what to do and that was all right cause she was the Ultimate Negress.

27

Story Twelve: Some Like it White although the Blacker the Berry...

My grandmama Obee didn't want my mama marrying this tar black boy named Melvin my mama was in love with. My mama said that Melvin could a been my daddy if my grandmama wasn't color struck. My grandmama didn't want us to come out dark. So when my mama fell in love with Bruce, a high yella with those fine white man features, my grandmama was pleased that her grand babies wouldn't be black tar babies.

Now of course my grandfather wasn't that light now. He was dark brown, on the verge of not being acceptable. My grandmama was light. Her mother was real light, Mrs. Glendora Tillman. I don't know their background. But we know some white man got busy or they wouldn't have come out caramel colored.

Anyway this color struck mess had folks dating and preferring white men cause not only was the babies gwine come out light-skinned, but white men was polite. Real polite.   Guess cause they grateful they got to taste somethang "exotic" without a whole lot of commotion, like sneaking some on 42nd Street in New York or visting poontang places without gittin' caught.

Any way for years I dated white, Puerto Rican, anything but black men and was proud. Bessie Smith had a white man. And so did that blues singer, what's her name? Named after a man...Billie...Billie Holiday. But here tell she fell fool in love with a black man.

Well I got myself a real black man and they said, "Once you go black you never go back." And, I know why. It's an awful thang for sure.

Well you know dem black men know everythang about their womenfolk. They know what hair weaves are, you just can't fool 'em for nothing or they act like they don't know but they do. They know who evil grandma and sistah are cause they live with 'em. They know how long chitlins take to cook. They're really into what is black. And ain't nothing like a proud black man. He ain't studdin' or puttin' up with no mess. And most folks know he mad anyway so they afraid of him. Afraid that he gon whupe somebody any minute.

Now a days light-skinned men got a problem, poor thangs. They just can't compare to dark toned men cause the blacker the berry - you say it "the sweeter the juice."

Story Thirteen: White Men

When I get tired of walking around in this 110 year old body, I work myself up, usually on a Saturday night cause that's when I feel wicked, a powerful spell to be 52 and holding. That's when white men chase me up the street. Of course Lord knows I can't decide what color hair I'm going to wear from day to day. So, sometimes I'm red cause I feel hot and then black cause it's time to be subtle and then of course blonde always mean I've gone stone crazy. When these white men see me coming with my beautiful bronze skin and face looking like Queen Sheba, they chase me down the street. At first, they are polite, but then they try to get you alone and then they are full of those hebe jebes and Lord ham mercy here they come.

Most white men just want black women as mistresses and maybe they love you enough to have babies. But, marriage is always just out of reach.

I must say there was a man, a white man, who was hopelessly in love with me, but I wasn't studdin' him. And you know why. Silly you might thank, but he smoked those stinking cigars and his mouth was all yellow and teeth stunk to high hell. Yes he did.

For a black woman to fall madly in love with a white man who doesn't really want her is just plain old foolishness.

So darlin' if yah foolin' with some man you ain't sure about be careful baby cause you know that mama and daddy don't like that interracial kind of mess.

It's so true that it don't matter who you fool with, who you love, what you do, if you love yoself enough you won't let harm come to you. You won't be out there givin' the store away! You won't let misunderstandings jump up without clearing the air. If you love yoself, you won't misuse your body.

If you love yoself, it just shows and everybody will know, including white men.

Story Fourteen: Harlem

Folks in Harlem got more sense than any folk in the world. They holler, they cuss, they fight and when they love you, they really love you. If you're on the outside looking in yah may think folk unhappy, but they ain't. They just pondering or minding their own business. That's what.

I love Harlem cause that's where I live and what I know, right up there on 122nd and Manhattan Avenue. White folks live right across the street too. They are Harlem folk, that's right. You don't have to be black to be Harlem folk. Don't worry me none that old color thang you folks always talking about. Anyway, when I go out in Harlem I change myself to be younger you know cause folks be rushing back and fro and at 110, I can't be bothered moving that fast and don't have to neither. Shoot I done done everythang I want to anyway. I ain't in a hurry to get nowhere no how.

Folks are worried about comin' to Harlem and they betta. There's some funky spirits up here just waiting for you to start trouble. You see Harlem is a village and the village is full of spirits. Most folks look at it like it's part of New York, but it ain't and I'm here to tell you so. Up here on 125th street folks are real and if they're happy, you'll know it, and if they evil, you'll find that out too. On 57th Street everythang look like it's just doing fine, but underneath that funky ground you got evil, angry thangs stirring up trouble every which away, just waiting, just waiting for yah to come uptown.

Now I don't know if you and Harlem gon get along. That's for you to see. But if you don't know where yah going, it might be betta to stay at home.

Story Fifteen: Once upon a time an Evil, Evil Fairy…

Once an evil, evil fairy had it out for me and what I did was bound that evilness. Yes I did. I got me the blackest candle I could find and had a long talk with my will. Every time that thing uttered something evil about me she drew one last breath until she breathed no more. Now, had the man left me alone, he would be alive and well today. I asked the man to stop being so evil to me, but he said that was his natural state of mind, evil. But he didn't know that I created that state of mind.

Don't mess with me.

Story Sixteen: The Cat Main

At first you might think the cat main is a man obsessed with pussycats. He's a man entrapped by the shapes, sizes and scents of the cat. He plots, plans and daydreams about how he can git the common as well as the rare variety of that mysterious creature, the cat.

But, I gots a different story.

Now there was a man who had only a picture of a cat, his cat, in his house, hanging on the wall. The cat's name was Sheldon. I'm telling yah the truth.

The man's name was Marty and he was a strange child. Now there was a woman desperate to be married so she thought Marty was strange but there was a possibility of finding a husband in this strange man. So what is strange she thought to herself. When she called the man, Sheldon, the man's cat talked to her over the phone. I kid yah not. Now that should a sent the girl packing (She was strange too? Don't you think?). But nawh — she wanted more proof that he wasn't stone crazy!

So anyway she got together with the man and he started to kiss and lick her face, and her whole body from head to toe like a cat. Lord child! The girl went crazy. When she asked the man where he learnt it from, he just smiled. He had a worried face but when he was licking, he looks like a little boy.

Well, she never got proof that he wasn't stone crazy cause love is blind, and the cat put a spell on her. She fell in love with the strangest, white cat you ever did see. She married the man, but the cat is her husband. Now you figure it out.

Story Seventeen: Sad and Lonely

Ain't no end to being sad and lonely while you alive, so just get over it and start living that's what. No matter how life seems to be going, it's gon be hard for you to stay in the moment and know that everythang is fine right now...and now is all you have. But you're human and humans like to worry. You worry worry. You worry about what you want and how you gon get it rather than letting things be. Worrying about worry ain't nothing to get worked up about cause that's what most folks do most of the time-worry. But, if you can let things happen, sit through your nerves showing out, things work themselves out. You can't control folk, but if they standing on your foot, betta tell them to get off it! That's all and that's what. If you want something from somebody, ask 'em, then see what they do.

Husbands leave and mothers die. That's life. Sad and lonely...sometimes.

If you have a hard time letting folks know what you feel, you might try getting honest with yoself. What are you afraid of? That they don't want to be with you? Find out now rather than later, that's what.

Everybody, even the evilest somebody want to be loved. Folks want love and that's all there is to it. If somebody is showing their behind, they want love. And, don't let nobody fool you, folks don't want to share their loved ones. Everybody's jealous. Some folks just know how to hide it.

Now just beware of what your loved one's folks were like cause they gon be acting much like their mama and daddy. So if their daddy is contrary, the boy gon be too

36

and if the mama sweet, the girl gon be too. Sometimes the boy acts like his mama and the girl like her father. Just keep those eyes open before you fling open the doors to your heart. Heed my word now.

Don't use your nature as a tool or something to bargain with or you gon get used. When you try to control somebody, you end up being controlled. So if you want to be free, let your partner be free. Sex and love are two different thangs. Remember that and you'll always know what to do when you have a question on whether you love somebody or not.

Womenfolk don't sleep with no man without a commitment. He must want to commit; you can't make him want to. That commitment will come from his heart otherwise, if it come from somewhere else, like his lying lips, it don't mean nothang.

Men seek love through sex cause they don't know no betta. They bond like women but even deeper if the woman gives him mother love and high nature. This is what they are hunting for anyway. Most women give too much mother love and not enough nature love to satisfy a man. You got to have both. They won't say it, but menfolk want to marry a woman just like their mamas. On a good day it's another way of going home.

Story Eighteen: Mrs. Fannie Mae Goldstein

Now, I inherited my altar and my apartment from an old, wise crone who lived 30 years in this apartment at 122nd and Manhattan Avenue. She was a high yella, pass for white gal, and knowed somethang from the day she was born. I figured wasn't no need for me to clean this place of evil spirits cause the evilest spirit in that house was her husband. She killed him off after she found out he was sleeping with another woman. That man got the strangest disease that no doctor could name and then he died begging her forgiveness. Fannie Mae Goldstein. She was black, Jewish, and proud too. That's right. You see in those days mixed folks had a level of respect they don't have today. Near white women marrying black men was an asset to the colored race cause they made light and bright, colored chillun. Any black man in his right mind marrying a light and bright woman was sho smitten and he shonuff had to have some money. That money let him do what the hell he wanted to do while folks were flapping their mouths. Of course his folks wandered why he couldn't settle down with a black woman, but that's another story.

Mrs. Fannie Mae Goldstein was a mess and being colored and Jewish was a heavy burden to carry. Colored, female and Jewish. Says it all, doesn't it? My Gawd that woman had to be strong. That's why she had to go kill that husband off with those herbs from Jamaica. The Negro bought her a synthetic diamond ring and she thought it was a diamond for 20 years. When she found out it was fake, she went off in a huff and wouldn't speak to the poor man for a whole year. The following year she found out that he was sleeping with a white woman. She was through then and that's when she slipped the deadly herbs to him in a Jamaican curry dish.

Seeing that she was Jewish that man wasn't on his job no how cause she was suppose to be a kept woman and she had to cook, iron and clean. Then when he lost his job, she had to wuk. What he do that for? She worked in a school in Harlem with poor chillun. Her heart was in the work, but her pride made her miserable.

Now Fannie Mae's father, Harry Goldstein, didn't give a hoot 'bout what folks said and after he made him a whole lots of money bootlegging he married Nell, the blackest gal he could find and had him three daughters. Nell was the Goldstein's housekeeper's daughter.

Everything after that is history. Harry and Nell had three children, all big boned, fine featured, good haired gals. They all married the blackest men they could find. Fannie Mae Goldstein was one of those girls. However, she was cheated out of her Jewish Princess heritage when Harry died cause in those days her mama, Nell, had no rights cause she was black. So when Harry died the Goldstein family swooped down on the money and disowned the children. But I tell you what, had Fannie Mae decided to pass for white and study that good book Torah, she could a been a Jewish Princess for sure.

Story Nineteen: Sex

You womenfolk give the store away when you have sex with a man without no commitment. Then you get mad at men when you don't get hitched. Some of yaw don't care about no commitment either cause you want to run loose like a buck stallion.

Now what you do is your business and ain't no need for me to meddle. But most of you just misery, that's what you are. You high natured and fast and think that if you give way to your nature like men you gon be betta off. But you finding it don't work out that way and it ain't in your favor. If you want to be happy you got to respect yoself and stop giving your nature away like it's every man's business to own. That's what. These days menfolk can knock on every door and it open. No wonder they just acting like fools and when a good woman comes along they say so what and walk on down the street to the flossie waving her behind around. Why should men get a yes every time they ask? For what? If you want somebody to value you, you can't just be standing there waiting to be picked up. That's cheap...that's just what I said gal.

All this fussing and fighting between men and women would be over if you women just kept your knees together long enough to get a ring on your finger. And another thang, all this equal power is hog mess cause the minute chillun start sucking on your breast, ain't no equality nowhere to be found.

Now if you mad about mother nature, don't worry none cause when you can't have no more babies, the man can't be making them like he use to either. He may think he

Casanova but the young women he trying to woo gon know the truth as well as you.

In love matters don't worry about what the man won't do. Just worry 'bout what you gon do when he get sure of you cause that's when men show their behind. Don't make the mistake and make that man Gawd. If you do, you gon be in more trouble than you can get out of. Remember a man don't pay no mind to what you say, it's what you do that stay on his mind.

A new man gon ask you a question three times...you know the question I'm talking about.

It is best if you answer No, No and No if you want more from the man than sex.

Story Twenty: Evil by Nature

Some folks just evil by nature. That's what they come here to do, keep up a whole lot of mess. Head doctors say all kind of thangs about folk like depressed, psychotic, chemically imbalanced, schizophrenic, alcoholic, and co-dependent when all a fool is, is just plain old country, low down evil.

Evil folks can't help themselves. They were born that way. You ever seent a baby not even one year old spitting at folks, hupping and hollering in the cradle and biting his mama's titty on purpose? And then have the nerve to smile up in her face spit just a drooling all over. And, every single Sunday just as the preacher start the sermon in church, at the same time, the child start showing out like he's evil and done sat down to dinner with Satan and his court.

You think I'm kidding? It's true chillun if you seen a day.

Just like the good lord sit down and have coffee and blueberry corn muffins, the devil sit down and have tea and biscuits. Evil folks got a right to live in the world just like Christian folk but don't nobody want to believe that evil folks carrying on just like they want to.

Well I'm here to tell you evil folk ain't studding good-hearted folk and they're in hiding cause they don't plan for good folks to take over the world. Evil is ready to party now so look out folks, here they come.

And, if you think I'm lying, if the pope won't bless Madonna's baby what is wrong with the world? And, where does evil live? What does that foolishness mean?

Last thang, if evil sneak up on you, walk wide-legged toward it like you carrying 16 inches of it. Squeeze your eyes up and say, "Were you looking for evil? Here I am."

Be evil and walk in peace.

Story Twenty-one: Diana and her Many Many Lovers

Now I once knew a child that was a big whore at heart and everywhere else. You get my drift.

Her folks made her go to Sunday school every Sunday but that didn't do no good cause her sap just rose right up in that Baptist church. Poor child her womanhood jest jumped ups one day and announced itself before she was ready. Truth was that she was scared to touch her clitoris cause her mama never told her what trouble would stir up there.

So when the child started bleeding her woman nature flew to the clouds. So naturally her folks called her "fast" instead of talking to her about what she was feeling. The poor child never got to make up her own mind about what she wanted. They just told her to keep her legs closed.

One day when she was about 13 and feeling grown she said to herself, "Now, let's see what boys do I like? I know I'm suppose to wait until I'm married to do it or do it to only one boy at a time, but I'm feeling mighty strong and all these boys look good and smell good too." So you know what happened.

The child got to be a whore just like that goddess Diana who had many, many, lovers both male and female. Diana didn't have no chillun to hold her back neither. All she wanted to do was hunt and make love. She figgered the men were doing it and she wanted to too.

Hunt and make love to as many lovers as her whoring heart saw fit to do-that's jest what this child Diana did.

Story Twenty-two: Bondage of Self

Ebea is a guiding sister spirit for me just like Hanna. In hinder day she was the most beautiful woman in the world, but only thang was she didn't know it, and she believed she was the lowest thang that walked the earth.

She suffered lifetime after lifetime where everythang she did felt wrong. You see that poor child was plagued by what you young-uns call low self-esteem. And I can tell you now it don't matter when it was cause if it was in BC or AD, the feelings the soul wears like a see through dress is all the same. That dress gon bound yah up even if others can see through it.

Nothing Ebea did was good enough. She couldn't even get it right in her dreams. And, she was sick from so many unnecessary thangs, like watching other folks' business and running after contrary men. Hell, she couldn't get enough business of her own going so she had to meddle in other folks' business.

So one day when she couldn't pick her head up from the pillow cause it was too heavy with grief, her grandmama, a Voodoo queen who minded her own business and had plenty of it, said "Girl if yah don't get up from there I gwine give yah somethang to cry about. And don't be messing around here cause there's enough mess coming up the road you gon have to tend to. Takes your behind out beyond yonder and bring me back some fresh onions and greens. We got to get ready for company." So Ebea went and did what grandmaw Tillie said cause she kept a switch hanging on the door just for whupping contrary chillun full of themselves.

45

After following grandmaw Tillie's advice, Ebea built herself up so high that she could not only help herself but she helped others just like her who didn't feel that they had anything to offer themselves let alone others.

When you tie yoself all up, the ground opens up and demands that you jump in it alive, all tied up and buried with blues of your own making. Ebea didn't have no blues except the ones she stored away in her head cause she had her health, her mind and loving folks tending to her cause she was a beauty queen in body but not mind. After following what grandmaw Tillie suggested she got busy and found the beauty of her spirit.

Being caught up in the Bondage of Self, low self-esteem, Ebea couldn't see that all along she was really free and beautiful, if she just let herself be.

Story Twenty-three: Curse of the Short Dick and Dry Pussy

Now I know you know that curses come in many forms, times and traditions. But the worse is when a boy's daddy passes on the heritage of a short, tiny dick.

Poor men they got short dicks. My Gawd what a life. Not enough penis to fill any hole. Lord, Lord. You know if I was a short dicked man, I think I'd just end my life when I found out what dicks were meant for and knowing I didn't have what it took to do it.

Personally, I feel Mother Nature is just plain wrong when it comes to womenfolk. After a woman done did her duty having those chillun and used those body juices to have those bleeding spells month after month, just when she start enjoying doing de do, her sap dry up. Imagine a whorish woman with natural flowing juices her whole life all of a sudden just done dried up. Look and see, gone. Spit won't even do.

When she begins to think of the juicy dick she once enjoyed, it now begins to hurt when she even fantasizes, because you know she only dealt with blessed men.

And, of course when you pair a short dick and a dry pussy, you got trouble for sure. Usually that happens when you got a little tiny man paired with an old big woman over 120. That's trouble and that's when the cutting begin. Cause you know on a Saturday night after he's worked all week long and stayed sober he ain't about to go and setup and look at no ugly fat old, ugly fat dry woman. He gon, with his short dick in his hand, look for something young and wet. "Praise Gawd" as the whoring deacons of Friendship Baptist Church used to say.

When that flat footed, short dicked man come in the house at 2:00 a.m. Sunday morning that fat, ugly old, fat ugly old, dry pussied woman gon have a fit. Cause we know that he got so mad at that evil woman during the week, and he got to stay sober for the boss man that he ain't using no fat old dry, when he can have some tasty young wet thang (course for a price).

But dry pussy got another thang coming for short dick. She got that funky blade she's been sharpening up for a long time. She's gon cut that Negro if the sun come out and if it never rain again she gon get him. Not for getting some young wet thang, but for making her put up with that short dick for 100 years!

Story Twenty-four: Black Woman StrengthSense

When everybody you know goes crazy and the world seems like it can't stand itself a minute longer, I bet yah some good old bacon fat, some black woman gon sit right on down in her rocking chair, light her corn pipe and say "So What."

That woman gon keep carrying on like nothing happened...cause that's black woman strengthsense. And although most of them are poor they got somethang you can't buy...they know what they know and they don't worry worry.

Black women are famous for their behinds you know, and that's the truth. But black woman got something more important than that derriere. It ain't nothing like the piercing thin lips of that white woman named Katherine Hepburn, or the silky white grace of that Sharon Stone, or the Fifth Avenue Tiffany "sumptin" of that legendary, white woman Grace Kelly. Black woman ain't never gon be in tune with fine white men like Cary Grant, even if Whitney Houston was rescued by Kevin Costner; that's in those picture shows. And lord it will be the day when Halle Berry never have to pay for nothing like that sweet child Elizabeth Taylor. But, one thang that the black woman got, neither white man, white woman or even black man have, is black woman strengthsense.

A black woman knows a nervous breakdown before it even starts, if it be in a cat, dog, child or adult. She seent it brewing; smelt it cooking. She knows when somebody's sick in the body cause she see that evil tint in the skin with her third eye. The woman doesn't have to spend a whole lot of time with a person to know what they're saying. She lay hands on the sick and heals them. She got a healing voice and will sing over you and pray over your food. She knows how to cook those collard greens that keep the body strong and the soul wise.

When death knock on de door and folks hooping and hollering she knows what to do, where to turn. This is black woman strengthsense, that's all. White babies done suckled at her breast when their own mamas ran out of milk. And the babies were stronger for it. Babies run to her instead of their own mamas cause they know mother love when they see it.

The black woman got soul intuition. Mother wit. Do you know what I mean? Strong black gal "no you won't, yah betta move along" common sense! And if a man try to lift his hand to her you know that hand ain't gon be no more use to him…ever.

You can't learn BWSS. Either you born with it or not cause you know it's passed on. BWSS let you know beyond what you see so you can say "I knows what I know and it's best that you don't mess with me."

Story Twenty-five: By Yoself or the Art of Isolation

Folks get on each other's nerves. They can't live with each other without hooping and hollering and keeping up a big mess about nothang! Menfolk need to sit down. Chillun are just fine until they start to smell themselves around 12. And you womenfolk with the new chillun just go crazy when the babies start hollering with those little mouths just a twitching. If they've been fed, if they're dry and if they ain't sleepy, well they just feel like hollering. Let 'em holler, good for the lungs and good so they can start singing the gospel early.

Womenfolk go through too much today...specially trying to figgah out what menfolk want. Do you know what you want? You work, you rear chillun, and you keep homes. You nurse a baby on one nipple and breast-feed a big old man on the other (cause he's probably jealous). You make half the cudbelly menfolk make and have more saved up for a rainy day than the flashiest man in a Cadillac.

When are you gon start realizing your worth?

You wives watch your husbands twist in circles at the young women who don't want 'em for nothang other than what's in their wallets. Just tell those young gals to make those men pay for every thang and make them pay good cause even old men cheat on wives and girlfriends. Some woman whether it's the wife or the mistress got to get him.

Less fighting going on between womenfolk these days. Good for you; I'm proud of yah. 'Bout time. I was worried about yah. Men got you fighting cause that's the

51

only way they can control you. If you get in one room together and start talking like you do today...there's going to be hell to pay and the men know it.

A self-respecting woman ain't studding no married man or spoken for man. She gon give the unseen woman her due.

Folks got to stop filling up on misery and start living that's what. Smart folks gon stay to themselves a lot cause they working on their own problems.

If folks make you sick, do a quick get away.

Ain't nothing wrong with being a loner with a life that's simple and quiet. Too much fuss, too many people, too much to stop you from pondering and whittling on your hickory sticks ain't a good thing. Contemplating yoself is important too.

Story Twenty-six: Miss. Rudolph and the Gluckin' Hens

Once there was a conjure woman lived up the hill right yonder behind my house in Tupelo, Mississippi in 1891. She raised hens that didn't gluck cause she let those women know that glucking hens got their necks wrung, quick and in a hurry on a bad day, especially if her corns was ailing. That way, all during the week when she was feeding and tending to them she didn't have to put up with all their hen glucking fuss. You see she figured they were gonna get it anyway, but while they were alive, they needed to be quiet.

Anyway, Miss. Cordellia, that was her name, sold hens on Sundays and that was the day the hens got to gluckin' cause they knew one of them was gon end up in Miss. Cordellia's skillet just a frying away.

Now there was one hen named Miss. Rudolph. Miss. Rudolph never glucked a word. She was ah unusual color for a hen too. Her breast was red and everythang else was black, even her eyes. Miss. Cordellia's husband, Yeller, that war his name cause when hog killing time came he yelled the loudest, told Cordellia that he seent Miss. Rudolph's black eyes turn yellow when Miss. Cordellia wrung the hen's necks. He said he thought that was a sign that that hen wasn't no hen.

Well what he tell Cordellia that for? She was 'spicious so she planned to wrang Miss. Rudolph's neck that coming Thanksgiving.

Miss. Cordellia wasn't afraid of no hen because she was born with a veil over her face and could see spirits and she knowned somethang from the day she was born. She told

Yeller to just hersh. Miss. Cordellia stop eating Miss. Rudolph's eggs. She started burying the eggs and every egg she buried, one of her hens died until the day came when the only hen left was Miss. Rudolph. That's when Yeller got scared and ran off with the juke joint owner's daughter, Miss. Lizzie. Anyway, Miss. Cordellia still wasn't moved and went into the hen house one Sunday morning with a hatchet. Well, ain't nobody seen her since, but we know that Miss. Rudolph must a kept on laying eggs cause on that same farm every which a away you turn, yah see black hens with red breasts and black eyes.

Story Twenty-seven: Grounded in Yah Female

If you want to be free and feel yoself be in the world, you've got to be grounded in yah female. That means you won't be afraid to be a woman grounded in her female.

A woman grounded in her female ain't afraid of loving and nurturing and when a man is wrong she ain't afraid to tell him so. And, if he leave, she being grounded in her female, know he be back cause he ain't gon find no home the likes of what she done made and shown him.

Now listen girl the home I'm talking about ain't a house. The home I'm talking about is your womanhood, your love, the way you make the man feel when you touch him and the way he feel when you make love to him. That's home and don't forget it. Don't forget that when he want to go home, he got to come to you. So stop all that fretting and worrying over that man and live what you know, and that is you...home...like you young folks call it...home girl.

Story Twenty-eight: Rich, Fine Deep Chocolate

Lord, honey Jesus in one of my lifetimes, and I was an old woman then, Gawd sent me the finest, blackest, deepest, sweetest, young black man. It was in 1922 in Buford, South Carolina. Lawd I almost laid down and died when I first seent 'em walking up the clay road to my house on the strongest, finest legs I ever seen. The minute that man kissed me, my toes started curling all the way back to my ankle.

But hold up now, he was young too. Just a young baby. I was 38 going on 80 and he was 25 going on 5 but he looked like he was 30. Remember when you know the craft, you keep yoself looking and acting young. I liked his smile and his readiness looking for love and he sho nuff found the right gal in me. I knew what a young black man like him could do for a woman like me, cause my sap was high and wasn't no one tending to it and he was craving to tend him a pussy willow garden.

After a few hours in the big old loving arms of a fine black man, whether you white, black, in between, male or female, you gon know what loving is about. You ain't gon be the same. Like they say, "Once you go black yah never go back."

The black man is full of passion and feelings. He been hated his whole life so when he get a chance to love...lord child watch out...he gon be expressing himself mighty powerful. Cause it's a way out for his pain and it makes him feel human again...not like some low down hound dog.

Now you may say to yoself why doesn't she get with men her own age. Well child, the truth be known, old men wore me out sistah with their fussing and complaining and set in their old tired ways. Old men just like to set on the porch, drank coffee and keep up a lots of mess in church, deacon mess. And they like to tell their womenfolk what to do every moment. I ain't going for that.

Now as you recall I told you 'bout my affliction and affinity to those white men. Wasn't my fault though. I'll tell you why. Black men got a lots to learn about how to take care of their women. Black women ain't going for that slave mess no more. They got their own money and if they gwine live for a man, he got to appreciate it.

Now I don't mean to be contrary, but you see too much mess with successful black men. First thing they do they want to get the whitest white woman they can find to help them feel better about themselves.

Then with that white woman, they start surrounding themselves with white. White house, white car, white butler, white secretary, and white money. As if that white gon make them white or brighten that black, never gon turn right face!

My Gawd the poor fool don't understand that he born black, gon die black, never mind what Michael Jackson done gon through. He unhappy with the way he look now any way.

A black man can appreciate what he is...fine, rich, dark, pungent chocolate...

Story Twenty-nine: Sex Me Up
with the Same Sex

Although I'm akin to the man woman coupling, I can't put shame on the love between men with men and women with women. There's somethang to be said about loving somebody look jes like you. So, men being attracted to men ain't nothing new.

Cause I speak my mind, some busy body told me that I'ma "homosexual man trapped in a woman's body." My answer is "So What." Just lets you know why I don't mind those menfolk that dress up like women and call themselves gay. Hell, what's wrong with being happy! And, so what if I feel like a man sometimes, cause many times how I feel depends on what side of the bed I get up on, the man's side or the woman's side.

The Chinese will tell you that everybody got yin and yang in them and anybody in their right mind knows that. So when a woman love another woman it's plain to see that one woman is the man and the other is the sho nuff woman in that pair. Nature is still showing her face but with a different kind of grin.

I prefer to be sexed up with the man. That man gifted with a certain manly walk and he usually bowlegged. If I was a man, I would still want a man which means that I'm still a woman, and that is why however it goes, I'm a "homosexual man trapped in a woman's body."

I recall a life as a manly man. I was a murderous soldier. I killed for money and was protective of women, children and the feeble. I was the finest, tallest, caramel-colored, hazel eyed, strong backed, well-endowed man with a sex drive drove womenfolk blind. However, I was chivalrous.

Having lived a life as a man and a woman it makes sense that you could come back again and be confused about who yah wanted, man, woman or both. So whether you sex yoself up with the same sex or the opposite sex, it's all good.

Story Thirty: This Life, Next Life

Once you've lived before and know it, everythang else that happens to you won't be so painful. You know that if you didn't get it right in the last life, yah might get it right this time.

There's a lots to learn each time your soul comes to do work. But many folks just lazabone and want to set up and gossip and tell lies about what they ain't done in a thousand years. Meanwhile, they've been setting right up on that porch dranking gut bucket gin and coffee, playing cards and trying to worm up under womenfolk skirts, or settle in men's back pockets, that's what.

So now when those same trifling spirits up beyond yonder start hollering about how they didn't "get it right," I tell them to just hersh cause they need to get busy and figger out what's wrong with themselves instead of the world.

Some folks like to stay miserable cause that way they can stay lazabone and blame everybody but themselves. Then you got some souls that really done some work on themselves, but that planet Saturn is mean and Mercury is fickle. The stars make it hard for them to overcome. That's when it's time to make friends with angels. That's what I said, spirits who've been through what you going through and are willing to help yah out. You see guardian angels ain't nothang but souls that done learnt their lessons.

And what are those lessons? The most impotent one is who you are and whatfore you here? If you are a lost soul, you gon waste time just being contrary, hurting folks and killing yoself with foolishness. Ain't nothang worst than having to skinarum inside a miserable, trifling head full of fear and hate. But overcoming this way of life takes raw heart in the kettle, which ain't no fun.

There are two ways to live your life. 1) Spirit dead like a fool with his head in his behind working up his nerves on what happened when he was a boogabug or 2) Soul alive conscious of your emotions and what fool is driving your bus so you free on that road to meet your maker. When you soul alive you always sweeping out the dirt in your house.

If you back here to get it right, it's important who's around you. If they trying to grow like you, that will work. But, if they living and speaking another tongue, check yoself cause sooner or later yah either join them or quit them. Now which one you gon do in this lifetime or the next?

Story Thirty-one: Wounded Chilluns

The world holding a lot of wounded chilluns. Sooner or later, if you gwine get on with your life, the child inside you got to be picked up, washed and loved back to health, that's what. You can't let that child keep getting hurt or lay in the mud for much longer. You grown now so it's time to be that child's parent yoself. And you can raise yoself different from how your folks did if it wasn't to your liking.

Now of course you got to set that crying child down and have a talk with her. Tell her that you love her and that you know that she's evil with you, but you didn't do the hurting. You tell her that the truth is that you and her are the same, and now you ready to take care of her from now on.

Wounded chillun lash out and kick and scream at everythang cause they can't forget what happened to them cause nobody nursed them back to feeling safe and OK with the world. Those chillun were seen and not heard so grown folks just ignored them. So all the jumping up and down and throwing fits makes the child feel good cause she gets the attention she never got. It's gon be hard for that child to learn how to sit still and be quiet.

Some chillun turn out to be evil, just plain old evil. Don't care about nothing that makes sense. The child is glued to pain in the soul and the spirit and she's gon act out.

When she acting out, you got to stay with her. Stay with her to let her know the nightmare is over and it's time to play. Give her a lot of toys like folks and love. In time that child will love herself enough to play.

Wounded chillun come on out and play now. Sowa say it's OK.

Story Thirty-two: Mr. Tittle

Mr. Tittle looks like a man but he's the biggest woman you've ever seen. His name is Mr. Tittle because he's got titillating tales to tell. That fool can talk some foolishness! And make you scream and fall on the floor. If you don't know what "foolish" is, let's stop talking right now.

Now Mr. Tittle likes to dress fine too and his favorite pass time is shopping on Fifth Avenue. All his jewelry is hand made or from that Tiffany store. Mr. Tittle is high yeller and proud of it too. Only thang he don't like about himself is that he's short but he says he's got girlish hips and that's what real men like.

The boy is a Virgo and counts money like nobody's business. I love to listen to his tales about growing up in the South, about white people, bout sissy sh_t and dangling d__ks and deep bu__e holes.

Mr. Tittle is what yaw call bisexual today. He truly likes men and women. I told him it's a shame cause he doing the women wrong by not having no babies and the men wrong by making them fall in love and stealing womenfolk' men.

"Never forget it baby, it's all about sex," says Mr. Tittle as he starts telling another titillating tale.

Story Thirty-three: Draw Down the Moon

Womenfolk need power and that's what those evil gals up near Purim do every month at the high moon...they are busy raising power. That's what. They are calling down whatever be setting up high on that moon cause they got bidness to take care of. Whoever done somebody wrong gon pay for sure, and if you ain't paid your dues and respect to these laundry washing, grease cooking hefas yah sho nuff gon pay when they through with the moon. Windy Willow asks me why I don't join in. I told her I'm too busy and I like to raise hell solo, that's what. Besides Windy Willow knows that I'm so evil I might walk up in that circle and burn it to high hell if somebody try to cross me or look at me the wrong way. I done lived so many lifetimes that I ain't got no more time to be patient with nobody. That's why my name is Sowa, means So What! That's what.

Anyway, those gals are right to do what they're doing cause the world don't have enough respect for woman work, like raising babies, cooking, cleaning and taking care of chillun and family. So the moon listens to the woman cycle and the sun takes pride when we full of child, the stars know when to birth and that great, great power is a woman that goes through cycles herself and she ain't studding no hateful menfolk mess for the most part. That's what I said gal. Listen up, that woman wants love and she ain't listening to much more.

So gal if yah don't know how to draw down the moon you better get busy and learn cause you out in the world with no power. But you don't have to start all over cause

65

you got the power but you scared of it and ain't learnt how to call it up, that's all. I'll teach you if you want.

Your candles have to be just so right, burnt at the right hour, that hour be your number, the day you born. Gal you have a responsibility to yourself to let no harm come to you. All this ill treatment of womenfolk would stop if you would just call down that moon together, that's what. If someone wants to hurt you, you bind them baby. Bind that evilness in a black cloth and hide it where it can't be found and gon about your business. When you see the bitsy say to 'em "Have a Good Day."

Now remember everythang evil takes care of itself. You don't have to do nothing. Same for good. Keep doing your good works and they'll come back to you ten fold.

The night gon be dark, ruby dark and love light will dot the sky until it turns the color of the third eye, purple. Those gals gwine be dancing on Purim hill, jes a singing and dancing under mother moon. Mother moon gon be wearing silver that night cause she feeling wicked right. Those womenfolk will pray over the womb where everythang starts. That woman cycle talks to the moon cycle and they converse back and forth, back and forth, until they reach an understanding on how thangs gon be. That womb talks to the moon and her story starts writing herself.

When womenfolk act like men that whole rhythm goes into an uproar and sure fire trouble starts brewing and ain't no stopping soon. The end of man as we know him ain't far behind.

Draw down the moon. Praise the sun. Turn your heads to the moon and get down on your knees and pray. Turn your mouth to the moon and howl. Lay your body down on the riverbank and be still. What you're asking for is coming shortly. When you see your face disappear before your eyes in the river water, know that you're home and ain't no need to worry cause your place in the universe is for sure.

Remember draw down the moon...

Story Thirty-four: Angels at the Gate

There's spirits, good souls, just waiting to help yah get through fields and valleys of your life. These spirits work through certain folks put in your life just when you need help through a "gate," the gate being a most powerful change like the death of a loved one or the birthing of a new soul.

You won't always recognize the angels but they're never far; you'll feel them. They often wisp right by you, you'll feel them brush against your skin and know that somebody is standing behind you. You can't always summon these angels, but rest assured that there's a loving power that rules spirits for the good of all. So mote it be.

Story Thirty-five: Love

Love is not sex and that's the mistake most folks make. When you're attracted to a man all you think about is how good he's gon make you feel when you lay down. But if you stuck on how you feel you're in lust and not in love. Love wants the very best for that loved one and a lots of time what's best doesn't include you.

Not many folks want to hear the truth about love because it's sweeter when it's a fantasy. Fantasies are sho nuff fabulous, but they don't last long. They're much like a picture show, they start and then they end so quickly that you don't know what happened. Same thang when you think you were in love, but it turns out to have been big old lust.

So what is love then? Well it's when you work in the field all day long and somebody's sick when you go home, and you need to go and get a doctor, but you've got to walk twenty miles when you're hungry and tired, but your loved one needs that doctor or they're gonna get real sick. So you walk.

Love is when you know you're so angry at the loved one that you just as soon bury 'em with a hatchet as eat a good, hot, home cooked meal when you're starving. But you call up all your will to act civil to the person and not wipe him off the face of the earth. That's what.

So love wants the very best for the person even if it doesn't include you. And, love is refusing to kill the loved one when you're kissing the thin line between love and hate.

Should you fear love? You dam skippy you betta if you in love with a fool.

Love is a potion mankind can't invent. You think of the "loved one" and get high. You want his breath on your face and his spirit in your soul. You want him to know your deepest dreams, and your evil fears. That man can smell you coming and you him.

If you fear love you might take what you get. But you don't have to, because true love will find you even if you running from it because love won't stop until it has its way with you. Just be ready when love skips through the door.

Story Thirty-six: Murderous Warrior

Now many dark African days ago I was a man and lived in a castle of my own. It was deep in the thick hills of what yaw call the Sudan.

I hadn't always lived there. I came to the Sudan with a Zulu king and I was his personal guard. We had a lots of enemies.

I knew how to get rid of an enemy. My biggest thrill in fighting was twisting or cutting a neck off cause it was fast and furious and I could move on to the next one before I finished the last.

My mama was an old wise woman witch named Rootsun. She birthed me when she was 82. She had a sister, Fray, who wanted to marry me as a child. They didn't get along and before long they was rivals for my affection. When Fray sent rovers in the night to kill my mama, I had to get revenge and kill my auntee. She was the only woman I killed and the only time I didn't enjoy killing. My ambitions to be ruler were cursed by my Uncle Botu. The rest of my life I killed folks for pay. I was a whore for anyone who would pay. Sometimes I would be convinced by a hire's enemy to work for him against my hire. If the cudbelly was right, I would. I didn't hurt babies, chillun or women ever. Since I had sent so many souls to hell, this was the only way I could live with my black soul. My killing spooked me but I couldn't stop.

I loved to kill.

I was tall, about 250 pounds with huge hands and feet, and a manly sized you know what, which I was famous for. Chopping heads off, stabbing rapists in the hearts, poking a

71

fool's eyes out was a good day for me. I wasn't hateful cause I had a freedom, murder.

I slept good at night. I ate hearty meals with a lot of wine. I seduced, bedded and loved many, many women. I was partial to virgins who I never raped, but persuaded with gifts and poems and the manly charms I could muster.

As big of a dog as I was, I never raped. I was a protector of women and with the vengeance of a violated woman, I castrated rapists for the public eye to see. My name was Zuvu.

Story Thirty-seven: Happy Haitian Whore

I was the happiest Haitian whore ever. And, maybe the most contented whore for hire who ever lived. I never doubted my worth. My worth came from my soul not my you know what. I possessed the sanctified musk flower of all Haitian time cause it rocked and rolled the lucky customer to another dimension. After that lucky man left me, he was good to go for at least three months, singing to himself, nice to his wife and kids and generous to his employees and peers. All because I gave him, for $100 ducats, exactly what he wanted.

I was in business for myself too. In addition to having that pungent intoxicating abode, I had an herb shop that sold herbs, oils, potions and spells for sale. I was not only a working whore but also a witch. Many troubled women came to me with their woman problems, man problems and money problems. I had answers for them all and answers that worked.

One woman in particular Sybil never seemed to get it right, no matter what she did.

"Seca, when that man gon fall out of love with that straying man of mine?" she asked me.

"When you bury two months of your menses and make sure that you put some of that blood in that man's drink and bath and he won't even remember that woman's name even less how she looked."

Well that fool woman thought that if two months of menses would get her man back, four would keep him forever. Well, when I give directions I give them for a purpose cause I know what I'm doing. The woman came back to me.

"Seca, when that man gon let me go. He ties me up at night so I won't move. I can't speak without him knowing what I'm going to say. I want to get rid of him."

I said to her "Sorry but I can't help you, you didn't do my spell, you did your own."

Story Thirty-eight: Revealin' Yoself

Revealin' yoself is a dangerous proposition if you care about what folks think of you. Revealin' that you a conjure woman and what you know is asking for more trouble than it's worth when your chest sticking out cause you think you got more power than others. You won't be going far with that kind of thinking, as far as the potion store and back. I know what I know and I'm what some folks call a witch.

I believe in Wicca and the old woman's soul religion. But I ain't no fool. I'm telling you this cause you can search high and low but you won't be able to find me cause I know what I'm doing and that's how to keep meddling evil folks out your way.

So if you tell folks where you coming from a lot of them will be evil with you and yah better know about binding evil and protecting your veil.

Revealin' yoself ain't for the weak or folks with no common sense.

Story Thirty-nine: Fear

What are you afraid of?

Of dying? What is so frightening about dying? Folks tell me it's cause they fear that they never lived cause they didn't have the nerve to be themselves and let the world know it. For sho it's terrifying to die having never lived.

What are you afraid of?

Of loving? Being as close to someone as you were to your mama and daddy. They let you down, didn't they? And, that loved one is going to too, some way, some time. But, what you gon do? Play it safe and never love? Let no one in so that they can't get to the part of you that will hurt. If you do that then love will never know you.

Letting it all hang low and loving and giving yoself to someone without fear is the makings of love. But you have to give from the heart and it feels like you are high and you might die. I know. But, that love is never lost and it'll always return to you cause you own the love that was given; it started with you.

This is Fear: You don't want to share yoself with the world cause you feel shameful.

This is Fear: You're bound up. You can't rise. You're afraid of what may be if you try.

Try this: Corner fear alone in a room full of light, tell 'em to gwine back in the closet where he lives and belongs cause you gwine live now.

Story Forty: Soul Mate

Oedipus, the son of Laius and Jocasta, was abandoned at birth. So he started out on the wrong foot with love. Oedipus killed his daddy and married his mama...mama was where he came from and where he always wanted to be. This way he would never be abandoned again, so he thought.

Whether you realize it or not your Soul Mate is the best and worst parts of your parents. And parents don't always do the right thang, even if they want to in their hearts. Only awareness that the way your parents loved you was the best they could do can set yah free to love whom you want to. What I'm saying is that you can forgive your parents and make a decision to love somebody different from them.

But spirits are creatures of habit and like to do the same thang over and over. That's why folks keep coming back repeating the same mistakes every lifetime. So most likely, whatever you do, you gwine fall in love with your mama or daddy.

He has strong big hands that heal every time he touches you. He has a big, big smile that always inspires you to smile. He is strong and big and gentle. So gentle.

Was she born on your mama's birthday? That ain't no accident. You know you probably conjured her up. Or you asked for him and your power sent him to you.

Soul Mates can't be explained, they just are.

Your emotions match and your neediness matches. Everythang works. You just are and ain't no struggle 'bout it.

Story Forty-one: Leave It Alone

Sometimes, not often tho, the blues will go away on their own. But you can't make somebody talk and walk against his or her natural, evil, constitution.

Leave it alone. Leave them alone. You can't force the sun to shine or the rain to stop when the bus, the train, the aeroplane won't come your way. LIA.

I once wanted this man, who was contrary from the beginning, to love me. He refused to love me "the way I wanted" so I just left him alone. I got busy with myself, turned around and here he come a galloping up the road as fast as he could.

Doggone it, by then I was done, through. Didn't want him no more cause it wasn't right from the get go.

Sometimes you find out that what you wanted just ain't meant for you and would be hell anyway. So leave it alone. It will take care of itself.

LIA.

Story Forty-two: Transference

Transference is one of those psychology terms that means you apply yesterday to today, one person to another, in error.

This is a dangerous thang to do. How you gon know what's real and what ain't?

Your life is run by old school days and yesteryear. Your lover, child, employer or lover of five lifetimes ago owns your heart today.

Who are you today? Transferring the past to today sho nuff won't let yah know.

Diane Richards

Story Forty-three: Shame

There was a beautiful woman named Vicky. She used to drink Robitussin, in those 1960's days, that fever medicine that contained codeine, and the doctor had to give it to you. She was a grand thief and a cheap call girl. She'd rather steal than hook any day. Vicky made friends with a young girl named Melanie. Melanie was young, foolish and fast and adored the ground Vicky walked on. She didn't notice that Vicky was a drug addict and wouldn't have cared much anyway. All Melanie saw was the time, attention and love that she got from Vicky. Vicky used Melanie to steal from high-class boutiques and clothing stores. But Vicky did other thangs too in her house. She sold her body.

Now Melanie was still in high school and she didn't want to get in no trouble but she wanted to impress Vicky with her willingness to learn so one night she agreed to spend time with a man friend of Vicky's. Vicky told her that if the man wanted to sleep with her he had to pay her $10.00. Now of course, Melanie didn't think that was much money, but she agreed to it anyway and was feeling mighty grown about the whole proposition.

Unfortunately and sadly Melanie turned one bad trick in Vicky's house. It was bad cause she gave up her precious innocence, womanhood, and do and didn't even get paid. Here now it's 30 years later and Melanie still ain't got over her shame.

That shame drove her to drink, drug and kill herself. The child's life went down all the way cause of one mistake. The mistake she made was not selling her body but holding on to shame until it killed her.

If she would a told somebody what she done and ask the Friendship Baptist church praying deacons to pray over her body, maybe she would a still been alive to laugh about not getting paid.

Shame for what? To change or to stay the same? If you gon live shame, it best be for change. But whichever way, in my book, shame is the only feeling not worth having. It will kill you won't it?

Story Forty-four: Courage

Courage is what you do when ain't nobody looking, that's what. Courage is somethang you have that you didn't know you had like when you got to jump up and fight for your life and you had no warning.

Courge happens over time, but some folks are born with it.

Everybody's got courage, but some folks don't know it and others got to be pushed to the wall to show it. Doing good works takes courage you know especially when you willing to pass up gold treasures to do right and you staring right at your neighbor who driving around in a Cadillac cause he busy doing evil works. Yeah, it takes courage to keep the good alive while the evil flourishes.

I was young more than once. As you know, I'm 110 years old now. But young once I was and I was a fool that's why I was fearless. Shoot if somebody was being done wrong I'd jump up and want to fight for 'em even if they didn't care for me. What was right was right. That's all and I didn't take for hepless folks being whipped.

Well let me tell yah a story about a small city girl with big city courage. Her name was Polly Shine it was. And when that gal smiled the world caught on fire with joy. Well she didn't like living in this small town in Kentucky so she set her sight on that big old, big, dirty, and low down city called New York. She was going to be a star! She got to that big funky city and what did she do? She got scared.

She had no daddy, no family, nobody. So the good lord knew that she couldn't just be in that big funky low down city by her so he sent her a white man look like John F. Kennedy.

Now only problem was she didn't like no white men and John F. Kennedy had him a wife (was working on his 2nd one) and a thousand and one chillun. And worst of all the man had yellow small teeth and smoked those funky rum soaked cigars. Every time he talked to her that funky yellow foul smelling breath came rushing out his mouth at her and she just about fainted. She had fainting spells I tell you.

So any who how, that taken into consideration, she had the nerve to allow this strange white man to take care of her in that big funky city New York. Now you know the gal wasn't right in her mind. She had picked up some floosie ways 'bout men. Make 'em pay was the stump of it. Give 'em a little and make 'em pay for it. Well only thing about that was that she had some fresh intoxicating stuff and the fool fell in love, lost his mind over her, left that wife and kids and moved in with her.

Polly didn't want that yah see. She wanted that man to stay put and take his flat white ass back to that hoof-n-mouth hefa in Katonah, New York and leave her alone with this fine young man she had hooked up with.

That's another story. However, I'll tell you this much, she didn't love that man either.

So get comfortable now. This is how Polly Shine found her some courage.

She war not right in the mind or soul and the evil part of her started singing and dancing. She got sick and started buying those donuts and cheesecake like there was no tomorrow. Stuffing her face as fast as she could she started to grow buffalo hips and thunder thighs.

However, Gawd had mercy on her and reached down into hell to get her out.

She had to choose between the menfolk. And, she did. She chose that man because he could do more for her than that woman. She wasn't all well yet.

Gawd gave that girl the strength and courage to make her way through evil living and thinking. She began to depend on herself; she got a job. Courage to change. She stopped lying. She got the courage to be honest. She started feeling good 'bout herself. Courage to brag on yoself when no one else will. She became proud of right living. She gave herself propers for being in the world and surviving. No matter who you are and what you do, you deserve respect. You live and die and yah deserve respect just for that!

And, you know what? That takes courage!

Story Forty-five: The Wicked Step Parent

Once upon an old Milwaukee brewing time there lived a stuttering, 6th grade educated man who spotted a beautiful plump but sexy maiden toting two little adorable angels. These angels turned out to be chillun from hell. This stuttering man's name was Clarence Greer. The maiden with two-chillun name was Glendora, and "Honey" was her nickname.

Honey wanted a laborer husband. Not no stuttering, needy, insecure religion fearing man. Clarence met Honey in Friendship Baptist Church. And, of course, Obee Toliver, Honey's mama, didn't approve of Clarence but knew her fast ass daughter was gwine run the streets if she didn't have no husband to tie her down.

Obee, being the grandmaw she was, was through with Honey anyway cause seem like every Saturday night she was trying to drop those caramel colored babies at her door and run the streets with Chickie, Obee's youngest baby sister.

Now looking back that Clarence got the short end of the stick. Those babies could never love him cause he stuttered, "Now, now now S-a-n-d-ee and and D-i-a-n-e I want my my tea with with l-e-m-o-n." First those gals didn't give a hoot 'bout what he wanted. He wasn't they daddy. He was too dark, stuttered, and the biggest insult was that he was a garbage man!

How could their mama, an uppity nurse who they were very proud of, marry a garbage man who picked up garbage in the white folks neighborhoods? And don't you know the poor man tried to be loving to those wenches when he

85

brought clothes from the garbage collections back to them. Lord hand mercy...!

Those evil ungrateful hefas hated him, especially that Rochelle. Clarence, Gawd bless his stuttering heart, wanted to love 'em and they mama from the start. But there was no way that was going to happen.

That southern grown son of Mary Flowers also had a peculiar smell whether he sweated or not. That stench stayed on the clothes the girls were made to wash in that new Maytag washer and dryer he had bought their mama.

Any who how, came a day when those two stepdaughters feared the stepdaddy cause he got mean when he realized those daughters were never going to love him like a father.

The girls liked his mama, Mrs. Flowers, cause she was kind and they liked his sister Brenda. They liked the way Brenda would tell Clarence where he could go and she made him stop fussing at those girls. Yes indeed Diane and Sandy liked that Brenda. She stopped plenty of whoppins in that house when she was around.

Clarence use to whop the girls whenever he felt like it cause he knew he wasn't loved. But it went wrong one day when Diane got feed up and tried to kick his ass for jumping on her mama.

"Now Glen... G-l-e-n.. you you ain't ain't going no, nowhere!" Clarence said to Honey threatening as she shined her spiked, black patent leather shoes and picked out some silky black stockings. Must a been that church-going deacon Clarence wasn't producing no honey under those sheets for Glendora.

As Clarence was threatening Honey, Diane was getting excited behind the kitchen door with her little face pressed tight against the door so that she could hear what they were saying. The girl had cue lines. The cue was the shoving noise and screaming voices. Diane would rush through that swinging kitchen door like a train screaming "Don't hit my mama!" Sandy would follow her. Sandy wasn't fearless like Diane. Diane didn't care if she was hit. Just as Clarence snatched Honey's glasses off her face, Diane would jump on his back clawing, screaming and kicking him in the back. Her little fists just a slapping at the man who smelled, stuttered and was a garbage man. Diane wasn't no more than 8 when she beat up her stepfather.

Poor Clarence Greer.

As time when on, Honey decided to have a baby with Clarence. Clarence and Honey had bought a new home in a white neighborhood and she was gon try to make a go of it...that is the marriage. Well, the gals loved, I mean loved that little black, curly headed boy named Jason. He was spoiled with three woman adoring him. But once again, Clarence was jealous. His need for love was nowhere to be found. And he resented that little boy, Jason.

Diane and Sandy got busy turning Jason against his father. Clarence got more evil and stricter. It was important for his adopted family to mind him and give him credit, more than showing his chillun that discipline was the way to success.

When Diane reached 12 she had been warning Clarence to back off her. She tried to tell him that she "wasn't the one."

One spring day, Clarence cornered Sandy in the hallway outside the bathroom and was taking his belt out of his pants to beat her. Diane had scared Clarence with her evil eyes, and snatching body. He had just about stopped giving her a hard time. She had his respect more or less cause not only was she the oldest; she would jump on him when he tried to beat her mama. She had put an end to his beating her mama.

So, when he pulled that leather strap out of his pants and went to hit Sandy, Diane rushed in front of her sister and with snake spit mouth yelled "Don't you ever hit my sister again! Don't hit me or my mama again or I'll kill yah!" Her body twisted up with balled up fists so hard you could see the blood through her skin. That stepdaddy knew if he so much as moved a limb to her if she could, she was going to kill him. Cause that was not a little girl standing in front of him, it was the devil herself who had lost her mind.

That was that and no more beatings followed. Two years later Clarence and Honey were divorced leaving the lily-white property to Honey and the chillun, which is what she, wanted anyway.

Unfortunately. Honey had to marry a stuttering fool to get ahead.

Story Forty-six: Mo' bout Red Gravy...

Now if you ain't figured it out by now I'll be straight with you child. Red gravy is about your self-knowledge and your ability to take care of yoself woman. You got to start honoring yoself above and beyond what you been doing. There ain't no room for compromise here child. Cook that red gravy whenever you need to say no. Whenever you doubt what you doing. Stop. Listen. Look through the windows of your heart and see what's going on in there.

Cook a real spicy gravy if you need to. When you start cooking look at the color of that gravy. Is it right? Do you have the right ingredients in it? Do you need more time? Do you need more love and tender care of your tired spirit? Is the heat up too high on that gravy? Are you going too fast with something?

Take your time.

Don't rush yoself or allow others to rush you. You understand what I'm saying baby?

Red Gravy is your own wisdom. And you got to learn how to cook it. I can't cook your gravy, only you can cook that gravy. I can give you the recipe just like that woman that came before me did. She gave me the recipe. But I had to learn how to cook my gravy. Now it's time for you to know how to cook your gravy cause it's yourn. But remember I'm here for yah. And I got plenty of different red gravy recipes.

Love yah, Sowa

Story Forty-seven: Sowa's Genealogy

Now I got all kinds of folks in my family tree and they kept up a whole lot of mess and had too much to say.

Most of 'em was foolish as me, but here tell that it all, the gnashing of the teeth, the tearing of the hair and the squatting at the bowels, started with my grandmama Mildred Beaubian, the Voodoo Queen.

Story Forty-eight: Voodoo Queen

A heap of trouble all started in Buford, South Carolina sometime before 1850.

Now my great grandmama Mildred was what they called a quadroon, you know when you so white the black folks can't stand you, and you too flavored that white folks scared you gon put something in their food. Well Mildred, knew what she knew when she got here cause her mama, great great grandma Beau put a hex on her slavemaster, Will Thompson, while Mildred was in her womb. You see Will had raped great great grandmama Beau and that's how she got pregnant with Mildred. Anyway, that hex made his feet swell up and his eye bleed when he thought about killing her.

Will Thompson didn't like nobody neither but my great grandmama Mildred. Didn't even like his wife, Miss Sissy Mae. And yah know Sissy Mae was out to get Mildred for sure. So there was my great grandmama all alone with folks hating her both colored and white. That's why she latched onto Ula.

Now Ula was the blackest, meanest, wet nurse on Will Thompson's plantation. Every baby she nursed grew up to be as evil as her. She didn't like nobody neither. Folks said she was into witchcraft and learned it from this African wise woman named Sister Mamee. I'll tell yah about her later. They say Ula used to make the moon bleed whenever she got with child cause the moon owed her some favors. When the moon would bleed, folks that tried to do Ula wrong got sick and died or begged her for forgiveness and that was the way it was.

Anyway, Ula took poor old Mildred in at thirteen when her sap was high and must a passed stuff on cause the next thang you knowed great grandmama Mildred was walking around with her head up high and those folks that hated her was asking her opinion and keen to do her favors. Even Ms. Sissy Mae stopped rolling her eyes at her and let her do work in the big house. But Mildred didn't do no real work other than work in that garden, which she liked to do cause that's where she grew all those herbs that she used in making gris-gris. Yes mam. By the time Mildred got to be 16 all the bucks running around including even her father Masta Thompson wanted to lay with her. But Ula was getting old and knew as soon as she decided to rest Mildred would be ripe for eating alive by her enemies. Ula said, "Don't be marring none of those fools that can't do nothing for you. And your own father looking at you ill like you ain't his own blood. You know the way now. I done done my duty. You got the secrets. Now use 'em. I plan to die in peace when you gone from here."

Well Ula meant all she said and when a free man's carriage visited the plantation to trade cotton, Mildred was on it. That carriage went right on up to New Orleans and great grandmama Mildred was taken in by some Creoles. Ula had taught her patwah and she passed for white anyway.

Being enterprising she setup her a store for gris-gris for colored folks and did fine white ladies' hair. While those white ladies were getting that hair done, they talked about they husbands and lovers and Mildred would always give advice that worked. So they kept coming back for gris-gris and hair fixing. Next thang you knowed between the coloreds' love and respect, the powerful whites that relied on her mudbone advice, and Ula's evil spirit guarding her step, Mildred became the Voodoo Queen of New Orleans.

Now of course she wasn't no saint and she had plenty of men trouble, jealous Voodum trying to hex her and bush priests trying to poison her and that's another story...

Story Forty-nine: Aunt Mamee – Healer Woman

Like I said Ula didn't like nobody because as far as she was concerned life was about being wronged. She hated white folks but more than that hated black folks for allowing themselves to be used like they were. But her mama, Aunt Mamee, put a stop to most of Ula's evilness when she taught her the secrets of Chara. Chara was a secret cult that only uncut African women from the Ivory Cost knew about. The Chara escaped from the heels and slashing of their menfolk and started their own tribe. They believed after you were cut all your power flew away. Of course, it took a long time before Ula trusted her own mama. Like I said she didn't like nobody.

Now Aunt Mamee had done something no slave back then had done. Somehow she left Will Thompson's plantation in Buford, South Carolina and made her way back to the Ivory Coast and got word back to Ula and all her chillun that she had gone home. Don't nobody really know how she got there, but folks say she conjured herself into a red crow and flew on back. Well after she cured blindness, mended bones without the white man's medicine and started storms with a blink of the eye, folks believe she changed herself into that crow.

After all that magical power, Aunt Mamee, all 300 pounds of her and those big dusty healing hands, was the kindest, most loving woman that ever came to Will Thompson's plantation. When she left, people would celebrate her going back home every year on St. John's Eve by dancing, eating and drinking like they was all about to die. Of course, Ula was the last to join in cause like I said she didn't like nobody.

Story Fifty: Catbone, The Bush Priest

Well with Ula not liking nobody, everybody was real surprised when she started waiting hand and foot on Catbone; a slave brought back from those Carib islands. But you see he wasn't no regular slave, he knew something. What he was, was what you call a Bush Priest. And the slave traders knew it too cause he wore this bone necklace around his neck and they wouldn't whope him. Whope everybody else, but not him. He would work when he wanted and rest as he liked. Shoot, he used to watch everybody work while he napped. He wasn't studding Ula neither. That's why she liked him. They got together and that's how Ula, with her Tillman hips, had 20 babies. Yes suh. Twenty babies and all from him. His name was Catbone cause he was evil as a tomcat and skinny as a bone. He could suck some neckbones. He'd suck all the grit meat out of a bone and then he'd take that same bone and use it in the snake oil potions he sold to folks in trouble with the masta, in trouble with the women and all kinds of mess. Catbone wasn't playing neither with Ula cause she tried to put a mojo on him to stop him from seeing other women.

As soon as she went to sleep one night he stood right over her, naked as a jaybird and manhood all sticking out with a dead squirrel turned upside down dripping blood in her hair and some white powder just a shaking over her body. All the while his eyes was rolling to the back of his head. Ula woke up, seent him, jumped out of the bed and started heading for the door like her behind was on fire. The door wouldn't open. That's when she hit her knees and begged him to forgive her. But Catbone didn't play that. He told her she had to cut off all her hair and go bare headed until he knew she wasn't lying. Well she did, and the sad part is that that girl's hair never grew back cause Catbone made it that way.

Story Fifty-one: Aaron, Son of Ula and Catbone

Well after a time, Will Thompson knew he had to get rid of Ula and Catbone cause they war too much evil in one place for him. Besides the truth be known he was scared of 'em. Will Thompson was so scared he didn't even sell them. He just told them one day to gwine on.

So Ula and Catbone made their way on and ended up in Louisiana sharecropping.

After all their fighting Ula and Catbone had a beautiful strong headed second sighted son in 1834 in Faraday, Louisiana. They called him Aaron. The boy was the first one that could read and cipher like nobody's business. But he had his father's temper and his mama's evil ways so you know he was something to reckon with. He was quiet reckon too. Only said something when it needed to be said. Despite staying to himself everybody loved him cause they knew he knew something. But the real reason is that Aaron walked with Gawd and even the devil was scared of him.

Folks say the devil use to come and visit Aaron and ask him why he wasn't scared of him like everybody else. Aaron just looked at the devil like he was a fool, folded his arms in front of him and said to him in a loud, ringing voice "Fool get your ass behind me, don't fool with me cause you gon be fooled." Then he went on about his business.

They say the devil stayed quiet at least a high moon after running into Aaron. Aaron wasn't studding nobody but his mama. He was old for his age and got set in his ways in his mama's womb. Ula even told folks that Aaron told her to be quiet when he was in her womb cause she talked too much.

But the most important thang to Aaron was his friendship with Gawd. Aaron started preaching when he was two. First words out his mouth were "Praise Gawd" and at four he was telling folks, "Fool be still and know that I am Gawd."

Now all this holy stuff didn't sit right with a certain white sharecropper named Samuel Ford lived right down yonder from Aaron's house. He didn't like Aaron when he turned his house into a prayer house and he hated that Aaron was planning to buy his mama and papa's freedom and their property. Gawd, Aaron's personal friend, blessed him day and night through his preaching and he was earning money through his growing ministry.

Aaron used prayer to grow the thickest most bountiful cotton while Samuel's ground scorched and dried up. One day at high noon Samuel stomped on over to Aaron's property and said, "Niggah what you know? What you doing to my land? You in cahuts with Satan!"

Aaron replied, "Naw suh and if you know what's good for yo ass you won't come around here no more accusing me of working with the devil cause I'm a friend of Jehovah even though I'll never be a friend of yourn. Cause I'm a uppity Negro and gon stay that way. And ain't no white man the likes of you ever gon talk to me like that again and keep his head. So get on the fuck off my propertee!" Aaron turned on his heels and didn't look back.

Next day Samuel set fire to Aaron's cotton. What he do that for?

They found Samuel Ford laying in his cotton field with his head resting on his chest, eyes turned up to the sun looking like he never saw a day. They say his head was cut with a newly shined up hand machete cause it look shiny and no one could find hide nor hair of Aaron and his family, even the house had disappeared.

Of course folks knew what had happened. Aaron had had a talk with Gawd...or the devil and the matter was settled between Aaron and Sam in a most Gawdly or ungawdly way, dependent on how you call it.

Story Fifty-two: New Orleans and a Black Greasy Skillet

So now Aaron, Catbone, Ula and the 19 chillun all settled in New Orleans in the early 1860's. But being family of slaves, folks had lost touch. So when Mildred, the Voodoo Queen, walked pass Ula they didn't speak cause it had been some forty years since they seent each other. Besides, Ula was so busy with a sucker nursing on her tit and two resting on her hips she was too evil to speak even if she wanted to. Yeah, she was barefoot and pregnant still at her old age.

Aaron didn't know that the Voodoo Queen was his mama's protege and what not. Aaron met a young woman named Lou Lou Bee. Lou Lou Bee knew everthang Mildred knew and more except she was trifling slow. Just plain old trifling slow and she didn't want to do nothing but sit around and eat, lay with men and get with child. That was her mission in life. When she did gris-gris it always did the opposite of what it was intended to do. That's why customers bought the opposite potion of what they needed from her. If they wanted to fall in love, they bought a fall-out-of love potion. Now, in spite of all this foolishness, Lou Lou Bee befriended Aaron and became like his sister. That's how Aaron met Obee.

Even though she was a big old Voodum, Lou Lou Bee sat up in church every Sunday morning praising and cursing the holy one just in case there was a hell. She was Obee's best friend. She used to tell Obee, "The good lord ain't thanking about you! You betta have a talk with Beelzebub." "What you know about Beelzebub, you can't

101

even make your gris-gris work," replied Obee sucking her teeth.

Obee was the oldest daughter of a preacher man named Reverend Tillman, and she like to sing in the choir and dress for church. Obee was young, pretty and proud. Aaron loved her sass and how she gossiped about folks and he didn't waste time asking Obee to marry him. He told her, "Listen woman, I likes yah and I'm serious. I want to marry yah and I want two dozen babies, all boys. Do yah want to get busy?"

Obee was twelve going on 40 and fast as all could be. She told Aaron that she might court him but if he was serious, first he had to talk to her father, Howard Tillman.

Story Fifty-three: Reverend Tillman

Now Reverend Howard Tillman was a big old proud black man and he just as soon whope you if you were wrong as sit down and have a cup of coffee with you. He got his temper from his daddy, Amos Tillman. Howard didn't play and he didn't have time to play. Between seeding 18 kids with Glendora, his freckled faced, light and bright wife, running his church, Philadelphia Baptist Church, and helping poor black folks come North he was too tired for foolishness.

Every morning at 4:00 a.m. he'd read his bible and go right to the Old Testament and read about King Solomon. That was his story cause King Solomon was blessed with more wisdom than anyone, had a thousand and one wives and plenty of gold to go alone with those fine wives. The way Reverend Tillman saw it, God was generous and he could be trusted. And, you didn't have to stop being a man to be a holy man. If you were tempted and your flesh sinned like King Solomon did, you could be forgiven. Because you see the truth be known, Howard Tillman was a ladies' man but he didn't want his life ruled and ruined by his manly weakness for pretty women. If he fell, he could rely on God to judge him like a man, still have a friendship with God and go on with his life.

When the Tillmans came north to Philadelphia from Faraday, Louisiana, they carried the name of their church with 'em, Philadelphia Baptist Church. There was a lot of Tillmans already settled in Philadelphia. There was so many Tillmans in Philadelphia that some unknowingly married each other.

Howard being the preacher he was, was asked to head up that Philadelphia Baptist Church and he drew a large congregation. When he first began preaching the church was just about all women. After hearing about that new, big fine black, southern preacher man in town, Christian women from all over Philadelphia would leave their fellowships and come on over to hear the gospel of the fine Reverend Tillman. He had to get married fast or all those "hungray" women would a cut him up, fried him up, and served him up like they did those Sunday afternoon chicken dinners.

Howard Tillman picked Glendora cause she was high yella, evil, contrary and wasn't studding him. Every other hefa was always in his face fussing over him talking about "Reverend Tillman it's a fine Sunday ain't it? You wanna call on me after church?" Naw he didn't wanna call on you. Couldn't she see he was tired after the sermon? Shoot he had jumped all up and down the pulpit, sweat flowing down, funk rushing out his arm pits. He was thirsty, hungray and tired. Listen woman gwine about your business he thought to himself. He wanted to go home where there was peace and quiet and no Walgreen's perfume, cornstarch and Vaseline smelling women trying to catch him in a hurry.

Howard was the first born son of Rose Tillman. Now Rose's husband, Amos Tillman, was lynched in Jackson Mississippi in 1933 for talking back to a white man. At that time Howard was 10 years old and he remembered clearly the night the Klansmen came riding high and fast to they house. It was just after midnight and the cotton was high around the house. Those white men burned the cotton first and then went and shot the horses in the barn and slaughtered a cow right in front of Rose. When they tried to rape Rose that's when Amos went berserk. He grabbed the rifle out of the leader's hand and shot him straight in the head. Then he turned around and shot two Klansmen who were trying to get away. That night Amos was a hero to Howard and Rose. But the next night as they was packing to leave town the Klansmen came back and snatched Amos right up. Hanged him and castrated him right in front of his wife and son. Rose started hurling out curse words so evil while they castrated her husband that the Klansmen was afraid to touch her.

They rode away into the night and heretell that every one of those men that took part in the murder of Amos Tillman all met death in the most unlikely way. One drowned in his own sh__t in an outhouse, another died having sex with a mojo woman, another sat down to eat sweet potato pie bought from a black church sale and died after the first bite. Yeah, Rose Tillman knew something and she slept well at night cause Amos didn't die for naught. And, she raised her son Howard to "neva be afraid of nanbody."

Story Fifty-four: Jack Leg Preacher
Mose Walker

Mose Walker was the tallest, 6'6", black African minister west of the Mississippi and boy could he preach. He would preach so long and hard that after the sermon folks would just either faint or start sputing the word of the Lord by heart. Yeah, Mose Walker knew how to preach.

Now Mose was one of those Jack Leg Preachers, yah know, he didn't have no home church. He would just tote that bible and those two pair of Sunday suits and shoes from town to town ready for that storefront Sunday morning collection. And you just know he had a special gold plate all shined up and ready for the coins and dollar bills church folks full of the "holy ghost" would gladly throw in that plate. Now they say Mose Walker was a distant relative of Aunt Mamee, the healer woman, and that he had healing powers. But, we can't be sure cause every time Mose Walker healed somebody, somebody died too. Some folks think it was cause he was in cahuts with the devil, but others say he just got to praying over those special medicines he made while he was drunk and would put the wrong potions in the bottles. So when folks thought they was drinking medicine blessed with the hands of Gawd's servant, they was really drinking poison made up by a drunk.

Another problem Reverend Walker had was he attracted those churchwomen like hungray flies. Those churchwomen would go dizzy over that man's black shining face full of the spirit. As he preached and started breathing hard and sweating they would get to breathing

106

hard right along with him. Seemed like they would just jump into his mouth and swallow every deceitful word he said. Look like they were fanning the heat off they bodies instead of heeding the word of God. As Reverend Walker jacklegged his fancy footwork in that pulpit, wiping that sweat off his brow and pointing his gold wearing hands at the sistahs, seemed like he was stirring up the work of the devil - pure lust I say. Lord hand mercy; just devilish lust like that devils food cake.

Now the menfolk didn't much care for Reverend Walker. They knew betta, but by the time they wives got through fussing about him, they figured they were better off by letting him come to town. You know he was famous everywhere and it was something for him to visit your town. You see the truth be known Walker had a tradition of bedding wit a couple of the sistahs after every Sunday sermon. And, the women looked forward to it, even though they didn't openly discuss it. So, Walker had been chased out of town a couple times by jealous husbands. But the husbands always played deaf and dumb the next morning cause they didn't want the virtue of they wives spoiled.

But one day Reverend Walker disappeared. And the story goes that one-week in late October of 1923, Mose Walker rode on in to Tupelo, Mississippi drunk and stinking to high hell. A church sister named Miss. Bernice, a respected widow, pulled him off his tired horse, fed him and cleaned him up. Now Miss. Bernice was an upstanding member of the Ebenezer Baptist Church run by Reverend Roosevelt Savage. Bernice carried Reverend Walker to church that Sunday morning. They say Walker got struck by the spirit of God and started speaking in tongue. But the problem was he was preaching in parable 'bout all the dirt he had done for the last 20 years. You see, Bernice didn't know it, but Preacher Walker was dead drunk. Well by the time he got through he had confessed to bedding just about every minister's wife from Mississippi to Louisiana. And you know everyone of those ministers knew each other. The men chased that man out of the church and had it not been for the women who loved that man's dirty draws, they would a lynched his monkey ass. "Don't spute my word," he said as he headed out of town on his tired horse. "I walk in the spirit of Gawd." But after all that you know those women talked those husbands into asking that man back...but they could never find him...some angry deacon or jealous churchwoman probably fixed his donkey ass in the end.

Story Fifty-five: Juke Joint Annie Mae

Now there was a very enterprising woman named Juke Joint Annie Mae. Annie had a hand built shack right out in the back of the woods outside Woodville, Mississippi. She made corn liquor by hand. Yes she did and nobody could beat her at playing cards. Folks didn't let her join in cause if they did by the end of the night they would owe her money for the card playing, the corn liquor drinking, and those hickory smoked barbecue dinners that she made on that wood burning stove setup right in the middle of that shack.

Annie's husband's name was Wallace and he was a white man. That's right. He had snatched pretty black Annie from her family when he first saw her picking cotton in Faraday, Louisiana. You see Annie was Aaron Toliver's sistah. What really happened was that white man had tricked her into coming with him to do some housework for some extra money. She believed him and when he kept driving and driving right on out of the state of Louisiana she knew either he planned to kill her or do the right thang and marry her. Annie Toliver was a smart gal and buttered him up, made the best of an ugly situation and the rest is history. After she got through wit Wallace he did everythang she wanted him to including getting rid of his red neck family cause Mista Wallace was in love.

Story Fifty-six: Sistah

Sistah was Aaron's first born. Now sistah was tough
and she liked to fight. She got that from Aaron and when
she got mad she twisted up her face just like her daddy use
to do to the man when he said "Pick that up boy!" Sistah
had a big old low-down laugh that you could hear from the
bottom of the house to the top and when she had her kids,
Sandy, Diane and Jason, she would call all of them at the
same time by the same name - SandeDianJason.

Sistah was the first one to wear an Afro. That's right in
1969. She came right on out of the house at 2512 West
Galena with that freshly washed head of naps proudly
displayed. She washed that scalp short hair of hers and it
"turned back." That meant you washed the grease and hot
comb out and that hair went jumping back to its natural
state - naps. White folks called it curls. But what did they
know? They never had to pull no comb through that head
at sunrise. Everybody with names knew that was fighting
time!

Sistah was loud, always had something to say, and she
war the class clown. She either beat your behind or made
yah laugh. As much trouble as she made for yah,
everybody still loved her. The eldest of the Toliver family,
she use to whupe her younger brother, Victor, like
nobody's business, but they were buddies and nobody
knew why. Now Sistah's mama, Obee Toliver, use to
whupe Sistah with a milk bottle and it never broke. Of
course Sistah never stopped her favorite pastime - fighting.

In grade school and high school Sistah got paid for
settling disputes. All you had to have was a quarter and
your troubles were over. She only had one true friend

named Etna Mae. Everybody else could be a friend or foe dependent on what side of the bed Sistah got up on cause she was a Gemini. She was smart in school anyway between her fighting and chasing boys. She caught her first husband, Bruce Richardson, right on North Division's football field. Sistah pointed her finger at him one day and said, "Hey you with your fine self come here. I want to talk to you." Bruce with his tall, lanky Puerto Rican looks shuffled on over to her. Sistah said, "You got a girlfriend?" He said, "No." "Well then you can just be mine," said Sistah. By the time Sistah got through making him laugh and beating him up, he proposed to her.

Now the day Bruce had to ask Deacon Toliver, my granddaddy, for Sistah's hand was the most terrifying day in his life and he'll tell yah that. Bruce spruced himself up, walked on over to the Toliver house on 12th and North Avenue, then turned on back to his home on Eight Street. He just couldn't face Aaron Toliver. You see in his eyes, Mr. Toliver was the most impressive man he ever knew about. He was a leader, a politician, a religious man and he was well respected by both white and black folks. So that's when his mama, my grandmama, Mildred told him that he came from Creole blood and that was the finest there was so don't be ashamed even if his father Sam, had deserted the family. So he went on over and faced Aaron Toliver and asked for Sistah's hand. Aaron said to Bruce, "Why do you want to marry my daughter?" Bruce told him that he loved her and that was that.

They had a huge wedding - the press, the Tillman and Toliver Clans, politicians, and the whole Friendship Baptist Church and Philadelphia Baptist Church congregations all came. That was my Sistah's day! She had gotten her childhood sweetheart. And of course they got busy and out came me, Sowa.

Story Fifty-seven: Baby Sowa

They say when I was a baby I used to look up outta my crib and point my finger at ill willing folks until they went blind and walked away. When they stop looking at me they would get their sight back. Anybody that wasn't supposed to hold me, when they went to try to hold me, they hands would catch on fire. That's right. Folks were scared of a little baby. My mama said I was so pretty that people wanted to steal me so she didn't trust nobody to baby-sit me so she even took me to work with her. She was a nurse so there was always a bed she could lay me down in.

Now when I was a child, about five years old, I told my mama that I was special and that I could stare right on up to the sun and not go blind. You see somebody told me that if you stare into the sun for more than a little while you would go blind. So I dared God to strike me blind. Of course, I figured God felt different about me cause I was special, and that I could stare as long as I took a liking to. So I went right on back out in my backyard at 2512 West Galena Street, 933-6823, and I stared and stared and stared... Then course I started to see a yellow light in my eyes.

I loved that light shining in my eyes yellow white, so bright and clear. I saw God resting in his easy chair just looking down on me. Happy to see me he was. I had a talk with him and we discussed my future. He told me that whatever I do I was going to be all right and it's true.

But now my sister saw me staring into the sun and ran to tell my mama. She said, "Sowa if yah don't quit now, I'ma a tell mama and now, so quit before you go blind." I refused to stop looking at that sun cause it was feeling good now and I felt God had reached right on down to me and

113

picked me up and put me on his lap. I was sitting on the lap of God and this girl wanted me to quit. What was she crazy!

Mama came and got me and picked me up. My eyes were wide open and I was having a full conversation with Gawd. Mama told me later that I was delirious and didn't even see her when she picked me up. I fell asleep and talked for three days to myself they said. But, I believe I was discussing things with Gawd.

Now you would think with this deep relationship with Gawd I was a good child. But I was evil, cause I was selfish.

Story Fifty-eight: Sowa

I've lived many times. Now I think I'll rest and stay put for awhile. I like my place in Harlem and those big old windows looking out on the corner of 122nd and Manhattan Avenue. That's right, if you curious about finding me you can go up on the corner and look up. Maybe see me and Crea, my pussycat. I'll wave to yah.

So I started out as a mercenary in Hannibal's Army, you know that man what climbed the Alps Mountains and invaded Rome. Then I got tired of fighting and wanted to do me some loving. That's when I came back as a Haitian whore. Don't form your lips to talk 'bout me. That's what I wanted to do and it was fun! I also was an African princess named Princess Taesh from that Ivory Coast, a blues singer in that Black Renaissance Harlem in dem 1920's named Bessie Richards. My evilness came out and I came back as a revolutionary in those 1960's named Angela Dabue. I changed up in the 1980's and became me a beauty queen and Hollywood black woman wit a white woman's soul. Yes I did.

But now child I'ma a resting. Yes, me and Crea and my corncob pipe and my rocking chair just a rocking back and forth, back and forth.

Now wait a minute if you wandering how I did all these thangs, yah ever heard of parallel time? I'm deep, ain't I? You bet I am so don't mess with me. If you knew who I was yah wouldn't be thinking like that or trying to look through this paper and see me like yah doing.

Story Fifty-nine: SowaFolks

Well it ain't easy being kin to the Richardsons, the Beaubians, the Tillmans and the Tolivers.

Now with the Richardsons you got those light skinned, educated, Creole folks from New Orleans and they southern upper class ways.

Then you got the Beaubians, real white folks marrying southern, black women and producing exotic southern fruit, black Frenchmen. Those Beaubians are somewhere in the Carolinas.

Now the Tillmans are some church going, chicken frying, whipping black folk from Mississippi. And pride, lord hand mercy, don't mess with them. First of t'all you can't get to them cause they head so high in the air.

Finally, the Tolivers are the fightenest, most contrary Negroes I ever done seent. They come from Louisiana and they don't intend to be lynched no more! Lord, don't cross them. They'll kill you on the road and then carry you right on up to the church pray over you and then bury yah with the Lord's Prayer and all. And, announce they serving dinner after the wake. Yessuh.

So that's where I come from...all those folks. Hmm. That's why I'm a strange one.

Story Sixty: Obee Toliver

Now Obee was a Scorpio and she married Aaron when she was only 12 years old cause she was "fast." Obee was next to the youngest of the Tillman girls. Remember Reverend Tillman had 18 kids, well Obee was next to the youngest. Obee loved to gossip, dress up and sing in church. She also could cook her hips off. When she met Aaron Toliver in 1929, he was 18 years old and just beginning to work on the dock up north in Milwaukee, Wisconsin. Weren't no black folks in those days to speak of or speak too loud, except Aaron Toliver.

Aaron Toliver took one look at Obee, the daughter of Reverend Tillman, a very respected man, and he knew she was his wife. And, he liked the way she sassed back to him, put her hands on her Tillman hips and told Aaron where he could go. No woman talked to him like that before.

Obee was pretty too with strong, thick black hair, childbearing hips and the proudest expression on her face you ever saw. She got that from her mama, Glendora. Her mama told her, "Listen gal don't ever look at a man beneath yah or that's what you gon turn out to be, beneath him." Naw, the Tillmans war careful about who they mingled with and who they allowed the girls to keep company with. When it came to getting married, the boy had betta be serious cause if you tasted the milk you was gon have to buy the cow, or you had to leave town or reckon with Reverend Tillman who was proud of his shooting and hunting skills.

When Reverend Tillman met Aaron Toliver he liked him cause he was in the church and an active, proud young black man. Also he heard the rumor that Aaron had killed a white man in Louisiana and he respected that cause Reverend Tillman knew a white smiling man could change into a white lynching man at any moment so it was best to be known as an evil black man. White folks could sense it and wouldn't mess with yah too fast.

Aaron became a union man active in politics and the church, just what a black man on the move was suppose to do. So, Obee needed some taming and in Howard Tillman's mind Aaron Toliver was just the one to do it.

Obee Toliver...

Story Sixty-one: Aaron Toliver

Aaron Toliver was a proud black man. His father's name was Ronald Toliver and he was a veteran of the civil war. Aaron was born and lived in Faraday, Louisiana. Aaron's sibling's names were Aunt Fannie, Aunt Clara, Uncle Bill and Aunt Annie. Don't nobody know much about Aaron's mama. Aaron had to leave Louisiana cause he murdered a white man. His brother, Uncle Bill, stayed on in Faraday and worked the land the two brothers had inherited. Uncle Bill use to send money up north to Milwaukee for Aaron to start off with.

Folks respected Aaron Toliver cause you could tell by the way he walked that he just as soon hit yah if you were wrong as shake your hand cause you wanted to be friends. He was a fighter, an organizer and a religious giant. He war tight with Gawd. He was a deacon in Reverend Tillman's Philadelphia Baptist church and later on with Reverend Hughes started Friendship Baptist Church. Reverend Tillman and Aaron Toliver became friends. There was respect there because they were the same kind of men - no fooling beat your ass black men dedicated to family and church. And, remember Aaron was married to Reverend Tillman's daughter, Obee. Aaron could a easily been a minister, but his interests laid in organizing men to demand betta working conditions for the dock workers in Milwaukee.

Aaron looked like that jazz trumpet musician named Louie Armstrong. His head was big and round and he had a thick black moustache. He just looked soulful. He had a big laugh and treated grandma Obee, like a queen. Obee never worked outside the home a day in her life. And the one time she did, she got mad at the white woman for calling her girl and walked out. Anyway, Aaron said Obee wanted to work cause she was nosy cause she sho didn't need the money. Obee dressed up in mink and pearls on Sunday to go to church. Uncle Victor and Obee use to discuss what she was gwine wear to church the night before. Uncle Victor would lay the clothes all out so she could be ready on time.

Aaron Toliver made plenty of cudbelly, enough for country ham, bacon, pig's feet, neck bones and collard greens with some black eyed peas and corn bread on the side, a little ham hocks and don't forget the hot sauce now. Obee Toliver didn't care about nothing but bearing Aaron Toliver's babies, raising them, going to church and loving her some Deacon Toliver. That was her job.

Aaron Toliver told his first born, Sistah, to go easy on her first born, Rochelle, cause she was gwine do much in the world. He must a known that Rochelle would fight with her mama as she struck out on her own. With doors slamming and a broom on her behind as Sistah stood with her hands on her hips hollering for Rochelle to get out of her house and never raise her hand to her again, Rochelle left that house at 4310 West 29th Street strong in her 16 years of pain. Soul Fire Craving.

When Aaron was alive the Toliver family was alive. They gathered in huge numbers for Easter, Thanksgiving and Christmas. And of course they had Memorial Day and Labor Day picnics.

But when Aaron Toliver died all that ended.

Aaron Toliver...

Story Sixty-two: Sam and Mildred

They lived in a white wood palace with those Victorian windows. You could see those white lace curtains just a blowing in the spring wind. But at night if you looked in that front bay window you could catch Mildred wringing her hands bleached white and dry from washing dishes and white folks clothes. All those dishes. Her dishes, other folks dishes, white folk dishes. But you know that gal was more than a worrier and washerwoman, she was a writer. But in those days wasn't no such thang as a colored woman writer no less making a living at it. Mo like you betta be happy just to be a married mama who could feed your chillun even if you would cry out in the middle of the night. Mildred. Beautiful, that high yella kind a colored mulatto from French blood. She married Sam. Sam Richardson, a man that looked like a knight. Had eyes so deep she could jump right in and swim in 'em. But his eyes were full of pain that nobody could explain and his mouth knew nothing but lies even though his heart was good.

That house where Sam and Mildred lived was on Eight Street right in the heart of white Milwaukee cause in the 1930's there was barely a Negro in town. That big old gentile looking, promising house was full of the blues. The kind a blues dragged your insides down to the ground and washed 'em red with guts and blood. Mildred didn't know where to turn and didn't know nothing bout cooking red gravy. So Sam put Mildred with child one night while her hands flew over her mouth in a desperate plea for mercy cause that man wasn't right.

Mildred had four chillun by that man that was supposed to be a knight - Charles, Bill, Betty and Bruce. Every child should a been blessed with a good fortune. But one sunny afternoon, Mildred stood on that front porch waiting for Sam to come home. She had baked apple pie, roasted some hen and whipped up some French potatoes and peas for the side dishes. That mouth full of lies despite a good heart never called and never came home. She never saw him again - alive.

Little Bruce who looked just like his mama never talked about Sam, but he never forgot his daddy. He loved that man so much it broke his little heart when his daddy went away for good. Sam Richardson passed for white and it seemed like to little Bruce with his father being a surgeon and all maybe he just ran away to be white and live in that white world. But Betty, a poet like her mama, knew the truth. Betty knew after her father had whispered in her ears and held her hands too tightly that he like the drink. Betty knew that more than any thing in the world her father loved the bottle. Now Bill, was a fun loving little boy and he use to drank right along with his daddy and loved it so when folks would call his father a drunk, Bill would ball up his fists as tight as he could and try to knock out the fool with the big mouth. And Charlie, well Charlie was like Sam, he kept everything inside and said nothing, but did exactly what he wanted to do. Charlie just made up his mind to quietly forget about the world. Anything he didn't like didn't exist.

So that beautiful picture of Mildred in her Sunday best and Sam in his army uniform standing in a rolling hill of peaceful grass was just that, a beautiful picture and little more. It was they very best moment captured in a picture. They were very, very happy - then...

Sam and Mildred...

Story Sixty-three: Jeremiah Bernstein

Now there was a little old Jewish man lived right on 135th Street and Lenox Avenue. I want you to know that this man was no ordinary white, Jewish man. And, I'll tell you why. Folks believed that he practiced white magic. Folks said he did cause all day long when he worked in his bakery store making that fresh chalah, rugelach and strudel, Lord hand mercy those were some tasty pies from scratch too that you ever tasted in your life, he would listen to people's problems. By and by folks would come and visit again and low and behold, those problems had just plain old disappeared. Jeremiah would wave his hand, shake his curly head and smile that tobacco stained smile and send the folk home with another tasty pie saying, "I told you all would be well with the help of God." Yes he did.

The reason I tell you this story, and that man was so special, is because nobody knew how many problems he had of his own. He couldn't sleep at night and often he would sob quietly to sleep just before he would have to rise to face another day. His health was failing although he was shonuff sprie on his feet for his age, and his own children had forsaken him in ways that no children should do to the father. But Jeremiah's work saved him. He loved to prepare the fresh dough and gather the fresh peaches, apples and berries for the sticky sweet rugelach. And, don't you know Jeremiah cooked some soul food peach cobbler and sweet potato pies that put that black woman Lenore on 145th Street to shame. Yes he did. Anyway, Jeremiah loved giving the children sweets after school when they would run past his store always stopping by to hungrily peer in the window. Even though their little dirty hands would smudge his windows the children made him happy in their innocent way of always greeting him. "Hi Mr. Bernstein," they would chime together expecting cookies right after.

One day a bad spirit moved into the neighborhood. He was a shaman if you ever saw one. He moved next door to the Bernstein Bakery above the Smith & Son's flower shop in an apartment that no one had inhabited for twenty years. Everybody thought that apartment was cursed because the woman who had lived there for thirty years had killed herself after her husband died. That shaman's name was Henry Tate and folks said he looked just like the dead husband of that woman.

Well that spirit turned out to be a thief, liar and maker of black magic for sure. Upon seeing Jeremiah the first time, Henry Tate spit on the ground. Jeremiah raised his hands to the sky in praise of his God.

After awhile, homes started missing valuables, divorces started brewing and children started going astray. When the children started missing that's when Jeremiah had a bakery sale day to remember. There were all kinds of steaming hot pies and sweet bread, smiling faces and children running back and forth under a Sunday day that went cloudy when Henry Tate showed up. But Jeremiah was ready. That evil ass Henry Tate bought one of Jeremiah's peach cobbler pies and a sweet potato too. Jeremiah sold those pies to him with a smile.

Well, need I say more? Nobody saw Henry Tate after that day and even his apartment above the flower store sighed relief and went back to looking like Henry had never set foot in it.

Yes indeedy. Folks started smiling again and they knew who to thank...Jeremiah Bernstein.

Story-Sixty-four: June Bug Eli Whitney

Now there was a boy named June Bug. That boy's real name was Eli Whitney, named after that white man what invented the cotton gin machine in 1793.

Now June Bug was a trifling lazabone lived in Tuskegee, Alabama born in 1827 from two parents. That's right too because you couldn't be sure back then cause you might not know who yo daddy was. June Bug knew who his daddy was and war not happy about it. Every time his daddy saw him, he'd pull out his belt strap and get to his behind. Why? Cause junior was always sleeping when he should have been picking cotton. Besides being naturally born lazy, June Bug had an ugly way of spitting and picking his nose. Yes, he did. His mama, Belle Louise Thomas, said he picked up those ways from the slave master, Runnie Rum.

Now everybody knew about Runnie Rum, that war his name cause every time he got to drinking that hot rum which he did every time he could, he'd get to stepping and then he'd go to running cause he couldn't stand himself feeling that good. He went plain out of his mind and the spirits in that rum made him run like something had got a holt of him, that's what.

Now one day June Bug was resting himself in the sun cause that's what he did and here come Runnie Rum plain out of his mind running like there was a bunch of spirits chasing his ass. He ran across June Bug's body like he didn't see it so June Bug turned over on his other side and kept right on sunning cause that what he do. Well that Runnie Rum ran around the June Bug again, stepped on his body and kept on running. Well it was around 12 Noon then when he ran around the second time. By two o'clock Runnie Rum had ran round June Bug about 20 times. Then June Bug noticed something strange. Runnie Rum was spinning a web like a spider around him every time he passed by. Only problem was that web was around him that's when June Bug wanted to get up and get to picking some cotton for sure. Wouldn't be no problem then for him to get to working cause his ass was trapped in that web.

Well come about four o'clock Runnie Rum started looking like a spider. His mouth was all twisted up spewing out some white sticky mess and June Bug was strapped down to the ground hollering and crying like he was going to die. Only problem was he didn't sound human. That hollering sounded like an insect. In fact that high screech sounded just like a bug...a June bug for sure.

Sowa Speak Handbook

Words	**Meaning**
ado	delay
aeroplane	airplane
aftah	after
akin	attracted to, in alignment with
bein'	being
betta	better
bidness	business
bodyskin	human body
bo	boyfriend
boo	loved one
boogalove	a Sowa term of endearment for loved one
boogarum	love
boogabug(s)	baby(s)
bosum	a woman's breasts, chest
bull	bull
buck	a man known for his sexual prowess
cain't	can't
cause	because
channelin'	when a spirit talks
chillun	children
connivin'	plotting
contrary	disagreeable
crainin'	straining your neck to see
crawdaddies	anxiety ridden thoughts
Crea	Sowa's cat

cudbelly	money
dawlin'	darling
dodarum	work
down home	from the south
'em	them, him
'emselves	themselves
enuf	enough
evilness	foul temperament
fickle	unstable
floatin'	state of being that is spiritual
for	for
folks	people
foolish	strong character, intrepid
Gawd	God
gettin'	getting
get	get
gahl	girl
gawn	going to
gon	going to
gonna	going to
gotta	have to
grandmaw	grandmother
grown	the state of being an adult
guardian angels	sperits (spirits) who have gone through hell and learned their karmic lessons.
gwine	go on

hair weave	woman hair fixation, compulsion to have better, longer, different hair from her natural hair
hefa	woman with a mean or sassy streak
hep	help
hisself	himself
holdin'	standing still
hoodwinked	fooled
hoopala	nonsense
huhself	herself
hussie	loose woman
iffen	if
impotent	important
James Brown	Soul brother from the 1960's who danced and hollered like a sex machine.
jes	just
lak	like
lazabone	chronic inertia, laziness
main	man
meddle	to intrude
meddlin'	to intrude
memba	remember
mess	trouble
messin'	to bother
mindin'	paying attention to
more	more
mojohex	sex
mudbone	down home
nanbody	nobody

nay	no
nothin'	nothing
nursin'	to draw breast milk inappropriately, usually done by an adult man
ova	over
ponderin'	considering
prancin'	to walk with a "dip in your hip."
'preciate	appreciate
preparin'	preparing
riff raff ass	full of sh..t person
sap	a woman's ability to bear children, sensuality
settin' up	sitting
sexae	sexy
skinarum	life
'spicious	suspicious
struttin'	to walk with an attitude in your stride
stuff	matters
sturrins	problems
sucklin'	nursing, sucking
suh	sir
thang(s)	thing(s)
tah	to
tahl	all
thank	think
tho	thought
they	their
tight red dress	vamp attire to wear when you're angry

thru	finished with your man, through
triflin'	nusiance
twig stick	cane
vuju	life and death
wanna	want to
war	was
Wicca	witchcraft, the worship of mother nature
wipin'	wiping
wit	with
without	without
womain	woman
womens	women
wuk	work
yah	you
yaw	you (plural)
yeah	yes
yo	your
yoself	yourself
young-uns	young people
yourn	yours

Expressions	**Meaning**
ain't studdin' yah	to dismiss you
all that	most splendid, larger than life
big old man	homosexual woman
big old woman	homosexual man
breakin' to a sweat	jumping on someone
cain't stand	to dislike immensely
carry on	continue
carryin' on	causing a fuss
clingin' like a ripe vine	obsession at its worst
don't give a hoot	don't care
emperor without no clothes	poor man that thinks highly of himself without merit
fool hearty	lacking common sense
from scratch	raw ingredients
give up the ghost	to die
goin's on	activities
gut bucket	raw, home made, strong
happy time	peace
hateful work	unsuitable work
head for de do	head for the door
heat up	become upset
hoopin and hollerin'	shouting, jumping up and down
in cahuts	to plot with someone
ill fixin'	bad intention
I' ma	I'm going to
in tow	following closely behind
it tis	it is
low down	no good, lacking morals

mack daddy	an insecure man who gains a false sense of self by selling and controlling weak women
mother duck	mother fuck
on them there	those
place your hand on	touch
pleasure womens	to make love to women
pot to piss in	homeless
put a fix on	to place a spell on
put upon	invaded, encumbered
raw heart in the kettle	courage, raw guts
reckon with	to make peace with
right hearted	a person with good, sincere intentions
small stuff	insignificant matters
somethin'	something
technicolor babies	children from different fathers and the same mother
that's what	just do it
too fit to be tied	overwhelmed, fed up
ug mugs	annoying matters, funky stuff
whole lots of mess	chaos
work out they nerves	act out on

133

Diane Richards

Food	**Meaning**
peach cobbler	pie made from peaches
peanut butter fried chicken	ghetto delicacy
pork butt fat	fat from a pig's hindquarters
red gravy	red ham or pork butt, flour, bacon fat, a touch of your big toe, Sowa's secret herbs given only to the right minded, concoction of southern wise woman wisdom

Remedies	Meaning
funk-you-up mint oil	oil to ward off all kinds of Voodoo, Black Magic and Mess
hemp root	hemp plant roots
red mint castor oil	castor oil with mint and a little red pork fat

Diane Richards

Sowa's Soul/Bodyskin Healin' Room

Come on in child and sit down. Tell me what's ailing you and I'll give you one of my soul bodyskin remedies. Make you feel betta 'bout what's bothering yah. Ain't nothing like a man problem to make your skin turn to crawdaddies or your feet swell up or your hair fall out your head. So now this is what I recommend for the following hurtings baby:

__The Hurtin'__	__The Cause__	__The Remedy__
Crawdaddies	__Betrayal__, Yo man done cheated on yah.	Make you some red moonglow rub. Rub it all over your body and then say that boy's name three times. Whoever that hefa was that seent him will be gone in a fortnight.
Shakin Fit	__Fear__, someone done put a mojo on yah.	Drink some Red plum tea. Fix yo lips just so to tell whoever tryin' to scare yah to say "Git the hell out cause I ain't the one."

The Hurtin'	The Cause	The Remedy
Blind Eye	**Uncertainty**, yah don't know which way to turn.	Git you some scleranthus herb. Try meditation and sit on down and do one thang at a time.
Lazabone	**Boredom**, yo loved one gone, your money low.	Git you some hornbeam herb. Exercise and turn off the picture shows. Find out what yah like to do and then do it.
Blue Heart	**Loneliness**, your loved one gone or yah don't want to be with him.	Git you some sweet chestnut herb. Git you the tighest red dress you Ever seent, put it on and go where the menfolks are. Call up a gal friend and ask her to go along. Git rid of a fool if you wit him. You cain't get the right man messin' with the wrong one.

The Hurtin'	The Cause	The Remedy
Knuckers	**Thin-Skinned,** everythang everyone says gets on your nerves. You cain't take criticism.	Git you some cerato herb. Git some larch herb. You want to start believin' in yoself even if yah fake it till you make it. Remember no one knows you betta than you do.
Cryin' Lutie	**Despair**, yah think the world gon end today.	Git you some mustard herb. Find out why you here and what your purpose in life is. Then get busy wit your purpose.
Looselips	**Caretaking**, yah so busy takin' care of folks that your own well bein' fails.	Git you some red chestnut herb. Git on with your own life. Stay off the phone and start mindin' your yah own business.